# HYDROPONIC MARIJUANA

## HOW TO GROW CANNABIS HYDROPONICALLY

# RICHARD BRAY

Published by *Monkey Publishing*
Edited by *Lily Marlene Booth*
Cover Design by *Diogo Lando*
Graphics by *Jamilk Assami*


1st Edition, published in 2019
© 2019 by Monkey Publishing
Monkey Publishing
Lerchenstrasse 111
22767 Hamburg
Germany


ISBN: 9781709369001

All rights reserved, including the right to reproduce this book or portions thereof in any form whatsoever except for brief quotations in critical reviews or articles, without the prior written permission of the publisher.

OUR HAND-PICKED
BOOK SELECTION FOR YOU.

# LEARN
## SOMETHING NEW EVERYDAY.

# Graphic Preview

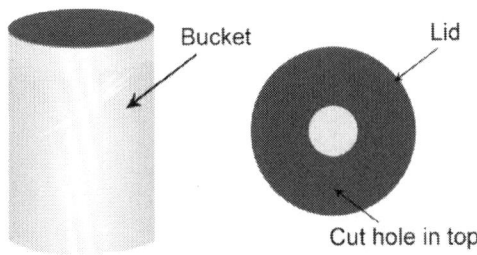

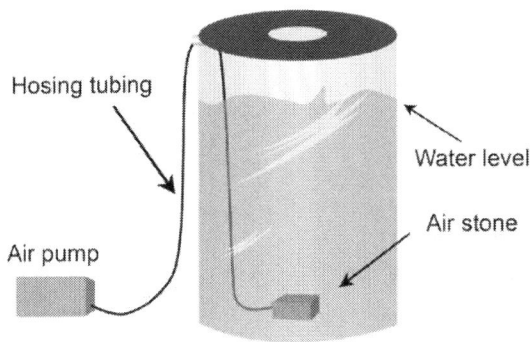

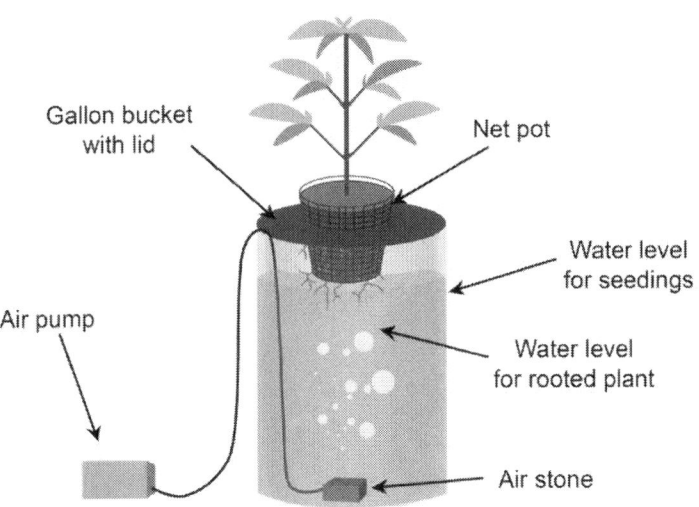

# Table of Contents

Introduction ................................................................. 1

**Cost to Grow Marijuana Hydroponically** .......................... 8

    Tips for Saving Money............................................... 9

**Plant Growth Basics** ................................................... 12

    Strains & Genetics .................................................. 12

    Seed Introduction .................................................. 15

    Male & Female Plants and Why it Matters ................ 17

    What Should I Grow? .............................................. 20

**Life Cycle of Marijuana** ............................................... 22

    Seeds & Clones ...................................................... 23

    Germination .......................................................... 24

    Seedlings .............................................................. 27

    Vegetative ............................................................. 27

    Flowering .............................................................. 28

    Harvest ................................................................. 30

**Hydroponic Marijuana Cultivation** ................................ 31

    Drip System .......................................................... 31

    Ebb and Flow ........................................................ 33

    Nutrient Film Technique ......................................... 35

    Water Culture ....................................................... 36

    Aeroponics ............................................................ 38

    Wick Irrigation ...................................................... 40

**The Best 3 Hydroponic Systems for Growing Marijuana** ................................................. 41

> Water Culture .................................................................... 41
> 
> Bubbleponics ..................................................................... 42
> 
> Ebb & Flow ....................................................................... 42

## Ideal Environment for Hydroponic Marijuana ........................ 44

> A Clean Space ................................................................... 45
> 
> Feeding the Plants/ Nutrient Solutions ..................................... 45
> 
> Nutrient Reservoir Upkeep ................................................... 52

## Growing Mediums ................................................................ 55

## Lighting ............................................................................ 60

> Which Light Type is Best? ..................................................... 63
> 
> Using Lights to Grow ........................................................... 64

## Air .................................................................................. 66

## Temperature ..................................................................... 67

## Humidity .......................................................................... 68

> Temperature & Humidity Requirements by Growth Stage ............ 68

## Equipment for Controlling the Grow Environment ................ 69

## Hydroponic System Set-Up & Growing ................................. 71

> Ready-made Kits vs. DIY ...................................................... 71

## Set-Up Instruction #1 - Water Culture ................................. 73

> Step By Step Instructions ..................................................... 75

## Set-Up Instruction #2 - Bubbleponics ................................. 80

> Step By Step Instructions ..................................................... 81

## Set-Up Instruction #3 - Ebb and Flow ................................. 90

> Step By Step Instructions ..................................................... 92

## Caring for Hydroponic Marijuana ....................................... 105

## Harvesting & Drying/Curing of your Hydroponic Marijuana Plant ..... 110

Flushing ........................................................................................ 110
Harvesting – Are My Plants Ready?.................................................. 112
Tips to Get Buds to Mature Faster .................................................. 116
Harvesting Cannabis, Step By Step .................................................. 118

# Pests, Disease and Other Problems ................................................ **128**

Pests ............................................................................................ 128
Diseases ...................................................................................... 131
Other Problems........................................................................... 132

# Conclusion ............................................................................................ **136**
# About the Author ................................................................................ **138**

# Introduction

Hydroponics is a reliable and easy way to grow Marijuana. With the fundamental knowledge provided in this book, you'll have all you need to start growing marijuana yourself. There are several methods for growing hydroponically and there is sure to be one that suits your situation and needs. Growing marijuana hydroponically isn't difficult. This book provides all the growing, caretaking, harvesting, and problem-solving information you'll need to have your own successful marijuana plants.

## What is Hydroponics?

Hydroponics growing uses a nutrient-enriched water bath to grow marijuana as opposed to using soil to grow it. This is very different from the customary way of growing using dirt, fertilizers, and water. In hydroponics, growing mediums are used to hold up the plants and all their nutrition comes from the water and from the air. This method is highly acclaimed because crops grow much faster.

In addition to growing faster, marijuana grown using hydroponics also produces higher yields, is easier to maintain and control, and delivers a higher quality product. Instead of depending on the fickleness of Mother Nature to provide sun, nutrients, and water, hydroponics bypasses all that and gives the plants exactly what they need, when they need it. The control is especially important when it comes to pests and diseases. In a hydroponics system, the chances of pests are almost eliminated. And, the closely monitored environment means that diseases can be caught with and dealt with before they become a big problem.

Hydroponics has been around for at least 500 years. The first book on the subject was published by Francis Bacon in the 17th century. Since then, there have been numerous innovations in the field; however, the basics remain the same. This method of growing can be set up indoors or outdoors. All you need is a basic understanding of how to set up your hydroponics growing system and you're off!

There are many ways to create a hydroponic system. You can either buy a kit or assemble it from scratch with your own equipment. Ready-made kits are a great option if you want to save time and energy and jump straight into the growing process. They also won't require too much explanation, as the process is fairly simple once you begin. So, while we'll cover ready-made kits, much of the book will be devoted to DIY hydroponics. DIY hydroponics is easier and more rewarding than you might expect, and this book will give you all you need to know to begin your hydroponic journey.

## Hydroponics vs. Soil

The main reason hydroponics is preferred over soil-based growing is control. When a seed is planted in soil, it relies on the organic material in the soil breaking down and providing basic nutrients. The roots of the plants then absorb the nutrients. The exact amount of each nutrient and element is hard to control. In fact, it is impossible to control soil completely because of potential unknown contaminants, biological imbalances, and not enough organic material to break down. When a plant is grown in soil, the plant has to stretch out its roots to find the necessary nutrients and then hope it is successful.

On the other hand, when a hydroponics system is used, the nutrients can be balanced precisely and perfectly for optimal growth. The roots don't need to search for what they need; it's all there ready and waiting for them.

Soil is also a host for pests, diseases, and contamination. Some of these you may know about when you use the soil and others you may be completely unaware of their existence. Hydroponics eliminates this guesswork and through the use of sterile growing mediums, provides a safe environment for your marijuana plant to prosper.

Since the plants absorb nutrients from the water and the air, the complete atmosphere of the hydroponic system needs to be regulated.

Using hydroponics to grow crops nearly eliminates the problems associated with soil-based growing. It isn't dependent on the weather; it saves space, there are fewer pests and diseases, and it's water and energy efficient. Most compelling, however, hydroponics gives higher yields and more reliable harvests due to its year-round growing.

# Pros/Cons of Hydroponic Marijuana Cultivation

**Pros of Growing with Hydroponics**

1. ***Grow where you may not be able to otherwise.*** Growing outside may not be a choice where you live because of a lack of space or too many regulations. Hydroponics opens up a whole new option for growing. Hydroponics systems can be set up inside in a spare room, in the garage, in a greenhouse, or outdoors. The flexibility is significant when it comes to deciding where to grow.

2. ***Efficient use of space and resources.*** Water, nutrients, and space are all utilized to their utmost capabilities. There is little waste of anything which means you get a higher reward for your efforts.

3. ***Quicker growth.*** Plants grown hydroponically usually have a much quicker rate of maturity. Quicker growth means faster harvests which are never a bad thing.

4. ***Control.*** You can give the plants exactly what they need when they need it in micro amounts, which means a healthier crop with higher and better yields. This is extremely difficult to do with soil-based gardening.

5. ***Grow year-round.*** In many locations, year-round growing is not an option due to climate and temperature. An indoors hydroponic system removes those issues and lets you have harvests regardless of the season.

6. ***Less threat of insects and disease.*** Insects live in soil. Diseases and bacteria live in soil. Hydroponics doesn't use soil so the majority of these threats are eliminated.

7. ***Less use of pesticides, herbicides, and fungicides.*** In conjunction with #5, pesticides are used to fight pests and a hydroponic garden has few of those.

Therefore, you won't need to rely on them as much or even at all. Herbicides and fungicides won't be necessary either without the presence of soil.

8. **No weeding!** No soil means no weeds.

### Cons of Growing with Hydroponics

1. **Cost.** This is the number one determent of hydroponics. However, depending on which system you use and how much you are growing, the costs may not be that much more than you need for growing in soil. If you plan a fancy hydroponic system, then it can get quite expensive, of course. There are many types, though, and you can find one to suit your budget.

2. **Knowledge.** This is something that you are overcoming right now by reading this book! There is a learning curve for sure. This isn't because hydroponics is difficult. It's simply because it's new to you. Once you've learned about it and gained some experience, you'll find this to be a non-issue. All things take time to learn. A person new to soil-gardening or anything in the world will have the same issues.

## Potency and Yield of Hydroponic Marijuana

There are a lot of factors that come into play when it comes to yields of hydroponically grown marijuana. Some of these include the variety, the size, the type of hydroponic system you are using, and your own expertise. Hydroponics, in general, will give you higher yields over soil-based growing but this isn't a given. Strictly speaking, if you plant a cherry tomato you will not magically get a big, lush, heirloom tomato. The same goes for cannabis. Hydroponics is not a magic wand. However, there are things you can do to turn that cherry tomato into the very best, highest yielding, cherry tomato plant possible.

Growing with hydroponics ensures that plants have the resources to grow to their full potential. In general, this means bigger, healthier, and more flavorful harvests.

The reason plants can't reach their highest potential with soil-based gardening is that there are too many variables that can't be controlled. The soil itself is an unpredictable variable. Bugs infiltrate it, rain falls on it, and animals scurry over it. All these things can impact the yields and you may not even know they are happening. In hydroponics, this doesn't happen. Everything that is needed to assist in growth, you are adding. There is nothing in the environment except what you bring in. All aspects of the gardening process can be micromanaged to the benefit of the marijuana plants.

**4 Reasons Hydroponics Gives Higher Yields**

1. ***Year-round gardening.*** In many places, this simply isn't an option because of the climate. The ability to grow all year-round greatly increases the number of harvests and therefore your yields.

2. ***Lighting is closely controlled.*** All plants need light to grow. Plants grown outside are dependent on the sun for light. The sun isn't always out, though. Cloudy days, rainy days, short winter days; these are all factors you can't control with outdoors gardening. Hydroponics has none of these issues and is not reliant on the fickleness of Mother Nature in any way.

3. ***Water is closely controlled.*** In an outdoor garden, rain, lack of rain, and inconsistent rain can have huge impacts on your plant growth. All plants need water and an even, consistent watering is best. With hydroponics, water is managed carefully and efficiently, giving your plants exactly what they need and eliminating inconsistencies.

4. ***Higher plant density.*** A higher plant density means more crops per foot and, of course, the more plants you can fit into a space, the higher yields you will have.

# Where to Grow Hydroponic Marijuana

One of the biggest benefits of growing hydroponically is that it increases the number of places that you can grow. You are no longer limited to inconsistent outdoor spaces with unforeseen circumstances. Hydroponic systems can be set up in a spare room, in a garage, in a basement, in a shed, or wherever you have a bit of space. It will depend on which type of hydroponic system you use but the places to grow will expand exponentially.

**Considerations When Choosing a Grow Space**

- Is there easy access to water?
- Is there good air flow?
- Is there easy access to electricity?
- What is the temperature in the space and can it be managed?
- Is there enough space for the plants to grow to their full height?
- Is there adequate space for the number of plants being grown?

# Cost to Grow Marijuana Hydroponically

The cost of growing cannabis hydroponically depends on which hydroponic system you decide to use and how much you intend to grow. There are some basic costs that you will encounter, regardless of system and size.

## Electricity

This is one of the biggest cost increases that may happen. A soil-based garden often uses the sun for light and heat, which doesn't cost anything. Hydroponic cannabis requires leaving grow lights on for long hours which can greatly increase your electric bill. Some soil-based marijuana cultivators also use grow lights so if you are already growing it like this, then the cost won't change.

Budget at least $400 for electricity over 4 months.

## Nutrients

The nutrient solutions needed to provide food to your hydroponic plants need to be bought. The cost can be significant if you are growing a large crop. Factor in at least $50-100 for a basic nutrient set-up.

## Lights

The cannabis plants will need some type of reliable light source. There are many options for lighting, some being more expensive than others.

The basic grow light set-up, which includes ballasts, bulbs, and hoods, ranges between $400 and $700.

**Grow Mediums**

While none of the growing mediums are especially expensive, it is a cost that you don't have with soil-based growing. The cost of mediums depends entirely on the size of your system and it can start to add up. Look for deals, sales, and buy in bulk! Costs for mediums in bulk range from $50-$200.

**Seeds or Clones**

There is no way around this one. Seeds cost money. And honestly, this is the one place where you shouldn't skimp. Get the best quality seeds you can because better seeds mean better crops which mean higher yields and better harvests. Invest in high-quality seeds or clones and you won't regret it. Seeds range from $10-$30 each.

**Fans**

The lights will produce heat that can negatively affect your plants so you'll need fans to offset this. You'll also need a fan or fans to keep fresh air flowing throughout the room. A good quality fan is important and of course, those are expensive. Budget a minimum of $100-$200 for fans.

**Water**

A hydroponic system depends heavily on water. It is the life-blood of the system. Water usually costs money and if you are using more than normal, then costs will go up. In general, hydroponic growing uses less water than soil-based cultivation methods; however, it is still a significant amount to consider.

## Tips for Saving Money

- ***Start Small!*** You don't need to create the best, most modern system the first time. Start off small and discover what works for you. You may find some of the more expensive equipment unnecessary. It's better to add equipment slowly than to buy it all at once and then discover you don't need it and wasted money. You may find that the simplest, least expensive option is all that you need to produce the amount you want. The Easy Water-Culture method is the simplest and least expensive option for beginners. It is the first diagrammed instruction set-up in this book and can be adapted for one plant or many. Starting with a simple system can save you hundreds of dollars on supplies, equipment, water, and electricity.

- ***Shop around for nutrients.*** There are a lot of suppliers of nutrient solutions online and in gardening stores. Look around for the best prices and take advantage of sales. Buying granulated nutrient solutions is less expensive than buying pre-mixed ones.

Additionally, many companies will try to convince you that you need all the different specialty nutrients in order to be successful. In reality, a basic nutrient mix is generally all you'll need, especially when you're just getting started. As you get more experienced, it can be interesting to test the different nutrient types but it isn't necessary. A successful marijuana crop can be grown with the basic nutrients. Only buy what you need and don't feel the need to get too fancy or specific.

By shopping around and only buying what you need, you can save $20-$30 per purchase on nutrients. This adds up after a while, believe me!

- ***Use auto-flowering seeds.*** These seeds grow and flower regardless of the light, humidity, and space you provide them. Of course, they will grow best under the best circumstances. However, when you use these seeds you don't have to invest as much in lighting and electricity costs if you don't want to. Of course, it will depend on the cost of electricity in your area, but potential savings could range from $100-$200.

- ***Buy previously-owned lights and grow room equipment.*** There is no need for brand new equipment. As long as it works, it's good. Look around online or on community sale forums to see if anyone is selling any. This is one of the biggest saving opportunities. Lighting equipment can really add up cost-wise and buying used could save you $100-$500.

- **Build your own grow box.** A grow box is a dark, enclosed space where the plants are set-up and the packages usually include all the lights, medium, and nutrients needed for the plants. They are used to regulate light, heat, air, and humidity and are excellent as an all-in-one buying option. Of course, the convenience costs money. If you plan on using a grow box, it's much less expensive to make your own. Basic grow boxes cost around between $100 and $300 but they can go all the way up to $1000+. Even including the time it takes to build one and getting the supplies, doing it yourself is a much less expensive option. They don't require a lot of building skills either.

- **Reduce electricity use.** It isn't possible to reduce electricity costs to nothing, however, there are ways you can save $5-$100 per month by being mindful of how you are using it. Using efficient lights goes a long way in reducing costs. Having an exhaust fan or fan pointed outwards reduces the need for AC if the heat gets too high. Arranging the plants at the right distance from the lights will also help with electrical efficiency. If the plants are too close, they can burn or overheat and that is a waste of electricity as well as harmful to the plants. If the plants are too far away from the lights, the energy isn't being used efficiently and more is needed to get a good result.

# Plant Growth Basics

Understanding the growth cycle of marijuana, from seed to mature plant is extremely important for success. Without this knowledge, it's hard to know if the plants are growing properly. From the beginning, the type of seed is important as it can dictate the way you need to grow. The genetics of a strain influence the percentages of THC and CBD in a plant. So, there are multiples of Sativa strains that are distinct because of their genetics which make their THC and CBD percentages vary widely.

## Strains & Genetics

There are two types of marijuana strains: Sativa and Indica. They are quite different from each other, with unique properties and characteristics. They require different growing conditions and vary in yield, size, strength, and type of high that they give you.

## *Sativa*

This strain originated in Africa, the Americas, and Asia. The different strains from each locale will vary, yet overall, they are similar in nature. The Sativa plants are tall, leggy, and have looser buds than the Indica plants, and grow fast. In general, they have significant THC values and give an energetic, potent, high. Sativa buds are usually fruity and sweet. Sativa strains give the classic marijuana "high" and feelings of happiness, excitement, and exhilaration.

## *Indica*

This marijuana strain originated in India. It grows bushy with tightly packed buds and dense harvests. The ratio of THC – CBD is very high with this type. It smells quite potent and the high is strong and generally relaxing. This is a common strain used for insomnia pain medication, anxiety, and PTSD. The taste is more intense than Sativa varieties.

## Ruderalis

The ruderalis strain is a low-THC variety or species of Cannabis which is native to Central and Eastern Europe and Russia. Many scholars accept Cannabis ruderalis as its own species due to its unique traits and phenotypes which distinguish it from Cannabis indica and Cannabis sativa; however, it is widely debated by many other scholars as to whether or not ruderalis is a subspecies of Cannabis sativa.

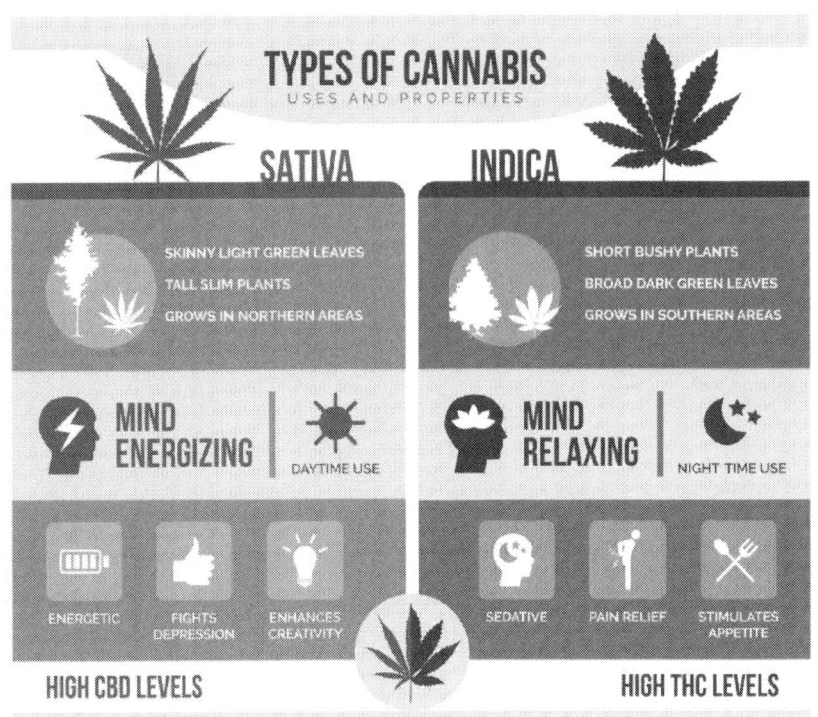

## *Hybrids*

The majority of cannabis seeds and plants are hybrids. It's actually quite difficult to find pure strains of indica or sativa. A hybrid is a cross between the two different types. The available strains of cannabis are widely varied with each containing a percentage of indica and sativa. Even though pure strains are rare, it's still important to know the two types so you can choose which one to grow based on the dominant characteristics. Over the years, there has been lots of experimentation with strains and genetics. A lot of this has been done by "recreational" growers and so there isn't always actual scientific specification as to what is exactly being created or sold. All of them will be some mix of indica and sativa, it is just hard to say exactly what the mix is. The majority of strains will say which one they lean more towards. A strain may be listed as mostly indica or mostly sativa, or a 50/50 mix or a

30/70 mix. Whether this is actually accurate depends a lot on where you acquire the seeds.

For example, the names of different hybrids can run the gamut and don't actually mean a whole lot. A seller can list their bud or seeds as Green Heaven, a name they just made up, and say it causes a certain type of high. The claims are largely anecdotal although, then again, that doesn't mean they aren't true.

When you are looking for seeds, be aware of what you are buying and whether there has been actual analysis on them. A strain that hasn't been analyzed isn't necessarily bad, it will most likely still grow wonderful cannabis; however, it's just good to know that what you get may not be exactly as described. Without a lab, it is hard to say the exact percentages of indica and sativa in each strain. If you are buying from a reputable seed seller, they should be able to tell you if the strain is heavier with indica or sativa and maybe even tell you percentages. If you are getting seeds from somewhere else, it will be hard to determine exactly which type you are getting. Likely, all that the seller will be able to tell you is what the high feels like and how the plant grows.

Seeds and clones are becoming more widely available as we speak, though, which means there will be a lot more regulation and continuity regarding genetics and strains. There will also be a greater analysis of exactly how much indica and sativa are in each strain.

## Seeds

The type of seed you acquire will influence the growing process. There are 3 types of seeds. Basic seeds, which come off the plant just like any other plant in the gardening world, can be used

to grow marijuana. Using these seeds though can be tricky, as they might not germinate well and may not stay true to type. In recent years, two new types of seeds have been introduced: auto-flowering and feminized seeds. Auto-flowering seeds make growing easier by allowing the grower to skip ahead in the growing process. Feminized seeds eliminate the problem of male plants negatively affecting bud growth and quality.

### *Auto-Flowering Seeds*

Introduced a few decades ago, these seeds have been a huge success. They begin flowering on their own as soon as they reach maturity, negating the need for you to trigger the flowering stage. This auto-flowering means you don't have to put the plants in separate rooms for the vegetative phase and flowering phase. They can all be grown together; plants of all ages can be combined into one space. An added bonus of these seeds is that they have a shorter vegetative stage and in three weeks they will begin to flower.

The auto-flowering seeds are hybrids of Sativa, Indica, and Ruderalis strains of marijuana. The Ruderalis strain comes from Eastern Europe and there is a lot of debate in the cannabis community as to whether the Ruderalis strain is a separate species or whether it is a subspecies. Either way, the strain is low in THC, flowering is based on maturity instead of how many hours of light and dark, and has adapted to the harsh, short, growing conditions of its native home. This is what makes it ideal to cross them to create auto-flowering seeds. When combined with the higher THC, higher producing, Sativa and Indica plants, this cannabis grows strong and quick.

### *Feminized Seeds*

Male marijuana plants are bad for bud growth on the females and therefore need to be removed. It can be hard to tell a male plant from a female plant, though, especially when you are a beginning grower. Often, by the time you can tell them apart, it is too late and the damage has been done.

Some very dedicated people came up with a solution to this problem and that is feminized seeds. It is also referred to as "cloning by seed" since the seeds are creating female plants closely identical to their parent. These seeds only produce female plants.

The process of creating these seeds involves causing the plants into a hermaphrodite condition through the spraying of a solution of colloidal silver, gibberellic acid, or through the Rodelization method.

While this type of seed sounds ideal, there are a lot of quality issues with producers of these seeds. It's a lengthy and expensive process to create this type of seed and not all producers take the time to do it right. This leads to a large amount of the so-called feminist seeds to actually be hermaphrodites which means that some may produce seeds. And that means your crop will be lesser quality and have lesser yields.

## Male & Female Plants and Why it Matters

Cannabis plants are either male or female. It is the female plants that grow the sought after bud. It is only female plants that you want when growing cannabis. Any male plants will pollinate the female plants and cause the buds to be filled with seeds. You do not want this! Unfortunately, it is difficult to tell female and male plants apart until they get to the flowering stage and by this time, if you don't catch the males quickly, it may be too late.

To be successful in identifying and removing the male plants, and therefore protecting your harvest, it is important to begin to look for the signs at the very beginning of the flowering stage. Check often until you are sure the gender of all your plants.

### *How to Identify Male & Female Cannabis Plants*

- Cannabis plants start growing "pre-flowers" approximately 4 weeks into their growth cycle. By six weeks, you should be able to see them and identify the gender.
- Pre-flowers grow in-between the nodes of the plants. The node is where the leaves and branches grow out from the stalk.
- Male plants grow pollen sacs that look like small yellow bananas and female plants grow stigma.
- It can be quite difficult to see the pre-flowers since they are so small and for this, you should use a magnifying glass.
- Look for the beginning growth of sacs (for males) or bracts (for females).
- Remove any male plants immediately!

## Hermaphrodite Plants

A hermaphrodite cannabis plant grows both female and male flowers. This is a natural occurrence among cannabis plants. It isn't good for cannabis growing, though. The buds will become full of seeds which greatly reduces the quality. There are some strains of cannabis that have a higher likelihood of creating hermaphrodites. An example of this is the Thai sativa strains and the reason is simply because of genetics. Before purchasing any cannabis seeds, read up on the strain as much as possible. Buyers will often list their experiences with the strain and if they had problems with hermaphrodite plants, they will say.

A plant can also become prone to hermaphroditic growth because of environmental factors. Stressed out plants will often become hermaphrodites as a way to self-soothe and ease their stress levels. This will happen during flowering if the plant finds the growing conditions too difficult.

**Environmental Reasons Plants Become Hermaphrodites**

- Light leaks. Interruption during the dark period during flowering. Any light during the hours of darkness, even the smallest amount, can be trouble.
- Overheating
- Damage to roots or branches
- Disease
- Nutrient deficiencies

The only way to lower the chances of your plants developing into hermaphrodites is to eliminate stress during the flowering period. Any pruning or growth training should take place before the flowering stage. The space needs to be kept sanitized, clean and monitored to ensure the plants have the best growing conditions possible.

**Identifying Hermaphrodite Plants**

- These plants develop both bud and pollen sacs OR they produce anthers which are exposed stamen that create pollen.
- Any time you know your plants have been under stress, keep an eye out for hermaphrodites.
- A plant that you have previously identified as female can become a hermaphrodite after being stressed out. Keep checking!
- Hermaphrodites can happen at the beginning of flowering, during flowering, and even after flowering.

## What Should I Grow?

As you can see, there are a lot of choices when it comes to the type of cannabis to grow and type of seed. Variety is a great thing, yet it can be overwhelming when you're new to growing the plant. One of the ways to decide is to simply grow what interests you. When you are starting out, there aren't a lot of "wrong" choices. Everything is an experiment and gives you experience.

## *Basic Characteristics of Each Type*

### Indica

Yield: High

Grow Time: Shorter

Plant Characteristics: Short and bushy

Effects: Relaxing, Sedating

Medicinal: Insomnia, Pain, Muscle Spasms, and Anxiety

### Sativa

Yield: Low

Grow Time: Longer

Plant Characteristics: Tall and slender

Effects: Uplifting, Energizing, Stimulating

Medicinal: Mood Disorders, ADD/ADHD, Depression, and Fatigue

### Hybrids

There are so many hybrids it is difficult to say which is better than another. The blending of Indica and Sativa traits and genetics can create a whole wide array of possibilities. However, knowing the traits of the Indica and Sativa gives you a better idea of what traits to expect with your hybrid if the developer says it is more like one than the other. The majority of seeds available today are hybrids with a leaning towards one type or the other.

# Life Cycle of Marijuana

Like all plants, marijuana goes through a predictable growing cycle. Knowing which part of the cycle the plants are in during the growing process is extremely important. There are different light, heat, and water needs for each cycle and to ignore them would impact bud growth in a bad way.

Seeds get their start with the germination process. This is what triggers the seedling to grow. After they germinate, they become seedlings and begin to establish themselves. Next, they enter the vegetative growth stage. During this stage, their foliage grows tall and fast. The flowering stage, which is next, is when the buds form and the plant is trained to focus on growing the flower and not the foliage. After the flowers have matured, it is time to harvest!

**Growth Stages Time Frame**

1. Germination – 24 hours to 7 days
2. Seedling – 2 to 3 weeks
3. Vegetative State – 2 to 3 weeks
4. Flowering – 6 weeks to 5 months
5. Harvesting

Compared to soil-based growing, hydroponics gives a much quicker life-cycle. The biggest differences are in the vegetative and flowering stages. The germination and seedling times are basically the same regardless of which method you use. In soil-based growing, the vegetative stage can last up to 16 weeks and the flowering stage can last up to 11 weeks.

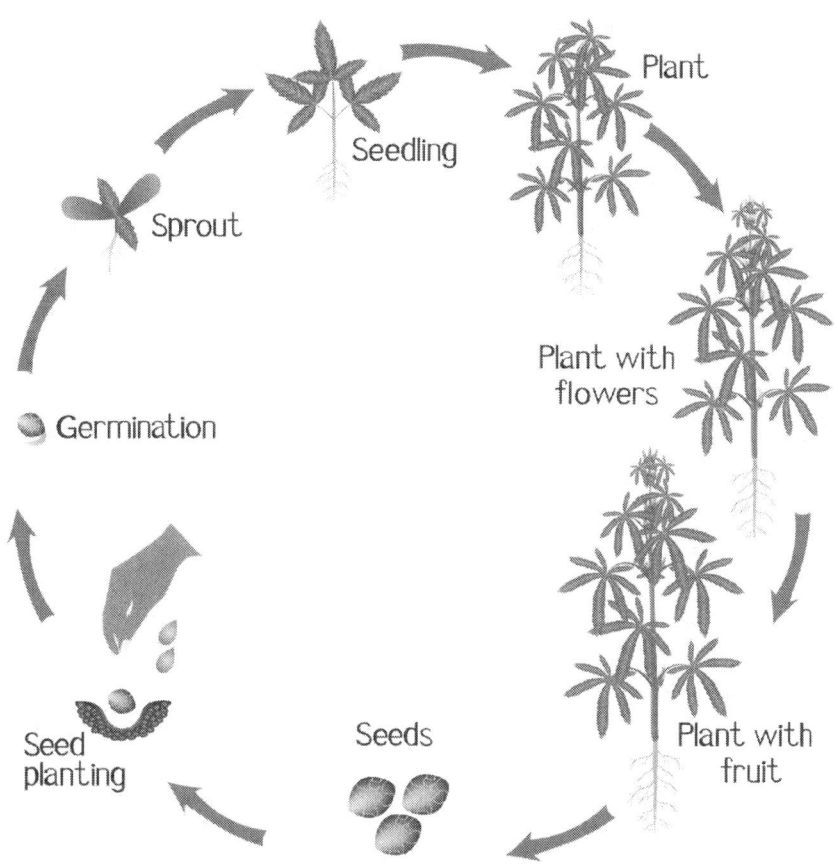

## Seeds & Clones

The seeds you use should be completely dry and hard. They should be light to dark brown in color. Green, white, or squishy seeds will not work. The most important aspect, however, is one that you can't tell by looking at it: Genetics. Always get your seeds from a reputable seller as there are many out there who will sell any seed regardless of whether it will grow a good plant or not. Good plant breeders take their time to develop a stable, balanced, productive strain.

Clones are another popular way to grow cannabis plants. Clones are cuttings that have been taken from a mature plant and then planted into the grow medium. Many people prefer clones because using them eliminates the germination stage of growing. Skipping an entire grow stage means quicker harvests!

Clone cuttings grow into exact replicas of the original parent plant. Seeds, on the other hand, carry the genetics of both the mother and father parent plants and when they grow you will get an unknown combination of the two. Two seeds with the same parents are unlikely to produce the same exact plant; each one will have its minor or major differences. Just like with people!

It goes without saying, but make sure if you use clones you know exactly what the parent plant looks like and how it produces. The entire point of using clones is to replicate the success you had with the original plant.

# Germination

Germination is the process of sprouting the seeds before planting them. Sprouting is successful when a little white tendril, about 1/8", pops out of the seed. This little tendril is called the taproot and all other roots in the lifetime of your plant will sprout from this root. The taproot will get continuously longer until it breaks the shell around the seed and pushes the seed upwards through the surface of your growing medium. Germination takes between 24 hours to 7 days.

The first leaves that emerge come from inside the seed. These are called cotyledons and were actually part of the seed in embryo. The next leaves that emerge after the cotyledons are called the first "true leaves" since the seedling has grown them on its own.

### *Four Requirements for Successful Germination*

1. **Moisture** – The seeds and growing medium should be kept moist without being soaking wet. If the seed sprouts and then finds itself in a dry place, it will die, so

be careful not to let things get too dry either. The seeds need access to water the entire time they are germinating.

2. **Warmth** – In nature, the seeds sprout in springtime. This is the type of warmth they need to sprout. High humidity is good too. A seed starter heating pad placed underneath the starts is a good way to keep them warm if you are worried about temperature. Do not let it get too hot. The seeds may be able to sprout in cooler temperatures; however, it will take much longer.

3. **Gentleness** – Use the utmost care when handling seedlings and taproots. They are extremely fragile and the taproot can snap off it handled. Try not to touch it and just handle the seed or stem instead, if needed.

4. **Peace** – Do not move or otherwise bother the seeds while they are germinating. They need a peaceful environment.

Do not start the germination process until your hydroponic system is set up and you know everything is working correctly.

## *Germination Method #1: Starter Cubes & Plugs*

Starter Cubes and Seedling Plugs are two tools designed specifically for starting seeds. They are simple to use, not too expensive and get great results. They both work the same way. There is a small hole already in the top of the Starter Cube in which you place the seed. Next, you pinch the top closed and then add water as directed on the package instructions. The germination rate using Starter Cubes or Plugs is very high.

If you are worried about the viability of your seeds, this is the best choice. Any seeds that may be considered old or not good candidates for planting could have a chance with this method.

**Using Starter Cubes & Plugs**

Place the seed on the top of your chosen growing medium and arrange the growing medium around it, keeping the seed in the top 1/3 of the medium. Do not bury it too deep. The growing medium does not give the plant nutrition; it's just there to support the roots once the plant starts growing. The necessary nutrients will be supplied from the nutrient solution. Submerge the lower 2/3rds of the growing medium in the nutrient solution being careful that the seed is not submerged. When the seed germinates, you will see a root growing out from it, about 1/8 of an inch long.

## *Germination Method #2: Paper Towel*

The paper towel method is low-budget, takes minimal effort, and doesn't require the purchase of any specialty supplies. The germination rates aren't as high as with the Starter plugs, however, the simplicity can't be beaten. The downside to using this method is that the seeds will need to be moved to the growing medium once they sprout. This is a very delicate process and can damage the seedlings.

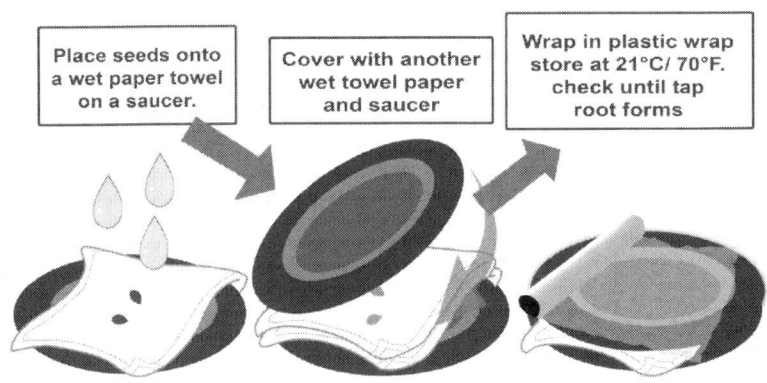

**Using Paper Towels to Germinate**

Tear off one piece of paper towel and then divide it in half. Moisten one piece until it is damp but not completely soaked. Place your seeds on the wet piece and place the other paper towel over them. Fold the paper towels together and slip them into a plastic sandwich bag. You can use a Ziploc bag instead of a sandwich bag; just don't seal it all the way. Place the seeds in a mildly warm location, between 65-75F (18-23C). On the top of a refrigerator is a good place. Let them sit, checking them carefully after 3 days for germination. It can take anywhere from 3-10 days.

Once they are sprouted, the seeds need to be moved immediately to the growing medium. The little tap root is extremely delicate and should not be touched at all. If the taproot falls off, the seed is no longer good. Using tweezers to move them helps a lot. Bury the taproot very lightly in the growing medium, just enough to cover it.

# Seedlings

After the seeds sprout, they begin to develop leaves. The leaves will be a bright, healthy, green color at this stage. It takes 2-3 weeks for the seedlings to grow big enough leaves to get to the next stage. At the beginning of the seedling stage, the leaves will have only one leaflet each. The number of leaflets (also called ridges) per leaf will expand to 5-7. They need 18-24 hours of light at this point.

The plants are very fragile in this stage. The roots are small and are vulnerable to diseases and to molds.

# Vegetative

The next stage of development for a marijuana plant is the vegetative stage. During this stage, the plant establishes a strong root system and grows like crazy. They can grow up to 5 inches in one day. It also grows full leaves. Plants in this stage need lots of light, 18 to 24 hours' worth. A timer is highly recommended during this phase so you can automate the turning on and off of the lights. Marijuana plants can be kept indefinitely in the vegetative state; as long as they are getting less than 6 hours of dark each day. Cannabis plants stay in the vegetative stage for 2-3 weeks until they begin to develop buds.

As the plants reach the end of the vegetative state, it becomes possible to determine whether they are male or female. Do not neglect to do this, unless you have feminized seeds and don't need to worry about it. Male plants can ruin an entire crop very quickly. If you discover any males, remove them immediately.

*Growing Lingo*

A plant receiving 18 hours of light and 6 hours of darkness is on an 18-6 light schedule. A plant receiving light 24 hours a day is on a 24-0 light schedule. When the plants move to the flowering stage, they are on a 12-12 light schedule. This applies to plants using artificial lights as well as natural light.

The specific light needs for your plants during this stage will also depend on the spacing between the plants, the temperature of the room, the efficiency of the lamps, and the reflectivity of the walls.

Marijuana plants need around 14% blue light during this phase to prevent them from getting too tall and leggy. Without the correct amount of blue light, the plant will be weak and have large gaps between the branches.

# **Flowering**

In a natural environment, marijuana plants will begin flowering in late summer as the nights grow longer. In a hydroponic situation, this environment needs to be replicated to initiate flowering. The plants get put on a 12-12 light schedule, which means 12 hours of light and 12 hours of darkness. It's very important that the dark time not be interrupted. After the lighting has been changed and the plants move to the flowering stage, it takes anywhere from 6 weeks to 5 months for the buds to be ready to harvest. The time needed depends greatly on the strain you are growing. The average time to harvest is 2.5 months.

Since the environment is controlled by the grower, flowering can be initiated whenever desired. The right time to initiate flowering is very subjective and will depend on what type of results you want. There are two main considerations when determining whether to initiate flowering or to wait longer, age and height:

### Age

A marijuana plant started from seed will not begin flowering until it is at least 2-3 weeks old, no matter what you do. A plant started from a clone can be moved to the flowering stage right after establishing roots. The reason for this is that a clone is a mature plant even when it is small since it was taken from a mature plant.

Some growers initiate flowering as soon as possible to keep the plants small and stout. This is called 12-12 from seed.

Other growers insist that a marijuana plant started from seed needs at least 60 days of vegetative growth in order to reach optimal bud production.

There is a lot of room for experimentation here and you will experience different results with different types and strains of cannabis. The bottom line: Switch the plant's light schedule when it suits you best.

### Height

Stalk and trellis the plants when they get to the flowering stage so the plant can support the buds that are growing.

In the first two weeks they are in the flowering stage, plants should be pruned. Do not do it any later than this as it can disrupt the natural growth.

A good basic rule of thumb is to change the light schedule to the 12-12 flowering stage when the plants have reached one half the desired final heights. Marijuana plants generally will double or triple in size during the flowering stage. This, of course, will fluctuate depending on type and strain of the seed. And, it also depends on how much space you have available. You may want to take measures to keep them short to fit in your grow space.

Ideally, you will be able to let the plants grow as big as possible since this means a bigger harvest. Of course, it isn't this simple. Maybe a quicker yield is more important to you. Or, the space makes a big impact on how you grow.

The flowering stage is much more sensitive than the vegetative stage. Mistakes made in the vegetative stage can be recovered from while mistakes made in the flowering stage can seriously affect your yield.

If some of the colas get too tall, they can be trained using LST methods (low-stress training). The colas are carefully bent down and away from the center of the plant.

For the best yields, it is recommended that the cannabis plants spend more time in the vegetative stage and are trained to fit into your space.

## Harvest

Once the plants have reached maturity, it's time to harvest them. Please refer to the chapter later on in this book to learn how to know when it's the right time to harvest.

# Hydroponic Marijuana Cultivation

Before we get started with instruction plans, we should have a look at different hydroponic systems. In this chapter, we will look at six different ways of growing marijuana crops hydroponically. Once armed with this knowledge, you'll be able to decide which system is best for your needs.

Of course, you may want to run more than one system, depending on the space available and how many types of plants you wish to grow. First, let's go over the growing techniques:

## Drip System

The Drip System is one of the most popular hydroponic systems. It's employed world-wide both for personal and commercial use. This system works well for growing marijuana. It's relatively simple to set up and works as an automated watering system for the plants. The draw for many growers is the simplicity in set-up and also that it isn't prohibitively expensive.

- Basically, water and nutrients are slow-dripped into the growing tray which houses the plant's roots.

- This system is ideal for plants with larger roots and for growing in hotter climates where water is sparse.

- As with most hydroponic systems, the drip system requires two tanks. One tank is the growing tray which houses the plant roots in a suitable growing medium. Beneath this is the reservoir tank, which stores water and nutrients and contains the pumps.

- There are two pumps in this system. One delivers nutrient-rich water to the growing tray from the main reservoir. This can be controlled by a timer switch. The second pump aerates the water in the main reservoir with the aid of an air stone.
- With the help of the air pump, air stones deliver many small bubbles that are filled with oxygen to the tank. While an air pump and tube can function without the use of an air stone at the end of the line, growers prefer air stones, which help diffuse the oxygen better than what the larger tube is capable of.
- The drip line is the tube which supplies nutrient-rich water to the plants. Liquid drips out of the emitters, which control the amount of water each plant receives. The water lands on the growing media and drains down to feed the roots. Each plant needs its own drip line.
- Gravity drains any excess liquid into the reservoir where it can be recycled. It is important to keep the growing medium damp. It should not be allowed to become either soaked through or completely dry.

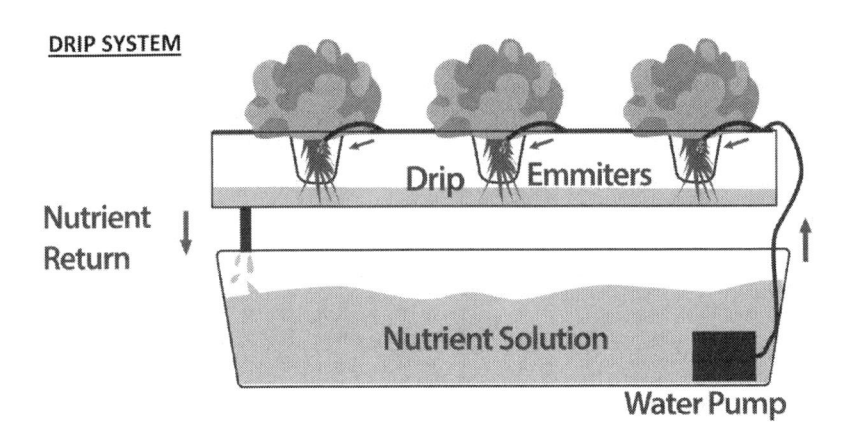

**DRIP SYSTEM**

Drip Emmiters

Nutrient Return

Nutrient Solution

Water Pump

The Drip Method can perform in one of two ways. It can be either recirculating/recovery or non-recirculating/non-recovery. The names of the systems are self-explanatory. They refer to whether or not the water is recycled.

- *Recirculating/recovery* systems are often used by home growers to keep costs down. The nutrient-rich water is not always used up by the plants. Rather than draining away, it returns to the reservoir tank via an overflow pipe. With this method, any water that collects in the bottom of the growing tray is recirculated through the system. The grower needs to check the pH levels of this system periodically. This is because nutrients will tend to become watered down in the recovery process. Also, the grower will need to top up the reservoir tank with nutritional solution from time to time.

- *Non-recirculating/non-recovery* is more popular when using the Drip System on a larger scale. With this method, excess water runs off as waste. It requires an extra piece of equipment called a Cycle Timer. This will add fresh nutrients into the main reservoir tank at timed intervals. Every now and then the growing media will need flushing with fresh water to prevent mineral build-up and algae growth.

## Ebb and Flow

This system also works well for growing marijuana. The plants have the nutrients delivered on a timed schedule and they love it.

- Also known as the Flood and Drain System.
- Popular with home growers.
- The medium that contains the roots is flooded at timed intervals. A flow of nutrient-enriched water is provided by a pump from the main reservoir, which again, sits

below the grow tray. Water then returns to the main reservoir through a gravity-powered overflow pipe.

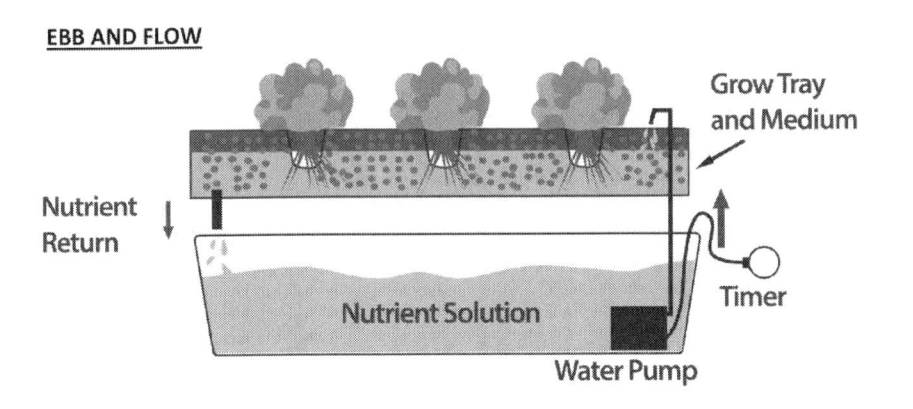

**EBB AND FLOW**

Here are some of the variations of the Ebb and Flow method:

**Tray Container**

In this method, plants sit on a layer of growing medium in a large tray. Nutrient-enriched water is pumped through a tube from the bottom reservoir into the growing tray. When the water reaches a certain level, the overflow returns to the reservoir below. One disadvantage of this system is that it can be difficult to remove individual plants as the roots can become entwined.

**Separate Containers**

Plants sit in separate pots, each containing a growing medium. The pots are placed in a large tray which fills with water. The rest of the procedure is the same as the tray method, with water draining back down to the reservoir. One advantage of this system is that individual plants can be removed easily because they are in separate pots.

- **Surge**

The main difference between the surge method and other variations of Ebb and Flow is that the reservoir tank does not need to be below the growing tray. There are still two tanks: the reservoir and the surge tank. The surge tank, which is at the same level as the growing pots, feeds the nutrient-enriched water via a pump. The growing pots are connected to the surge tank via pipes that sit below the water line.

The principle is that the water in the surge tank is at the same level as it is in the growing pots. When the water in the surge tank reaches a certain level, a pump is activated. This returns the water to the main tank. As the water in the surge tank drops, so does the water in the growing pots. This system is more expensive to construct as there are more parts required.

The size of your water pump depends on the design of your hydroponic system. It is advisable to get a bigger pump than you actually think you'll need, because you can always reduce the water flow but not vice versa. You can use simple submersible fountain and pond pumps for your hydroponic system.

## Nutrient Film Technique

This method works great for growing marijuana, however, it takes more skill and expertise to set it up and maintain it. It's not usually the best choice for new growers.

- Ideal for small, quick-growing plants.
- The reservoir tank sits underneath the growing compartments and contains nutrient-enriched water. This water is pumped to separate grow channels.
- The growing compartments are usually gullies or tubes that allow the water to flow through. Plants sit in a basket on the tray with their roots suspended through a hole. This method allows the roots to access the nutritional flow of water in the bottom of the gully.

- Nutrient-enriched water is pumped up through a tube. It enters one end of a growing channel which sits on an angle. Water flows down the slope and returns through a waste pipe situated at the other end of the gullies. The roots act like a wick and soak up the liquid.
- The method requires accurate measurements of flow rate and correct slant angle in order to be effective.
- The flow is constant, so the pump must active at all times.
- Roots are more exposed in this system. Because of this, it's important to monitor humidity and temperature levels. If you don't, the roots could dry out or become waterlogged, which could result in the loss of the entire crop.
- Watch out for roots clogging the system and blocking the water flow.

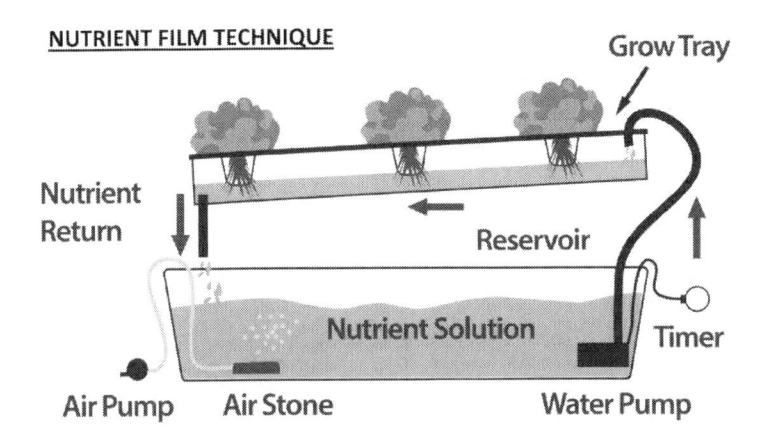

**NUTRIENT FILM TECHNIQUE**

## Water Culture

This is the most popular method by far for growing cannabis hydroponically. It's easy to set-up, isn't expensive or complicated to build, and there are many adaptations that can be made to suit individual situations. A variation of Water Culture called Bubbleponics is especially well-suited for cannabis growing.

- Popular for commercial farming as it's an inexpensive method for large-scale usage. It's equally as popular with the smaller homesteaders because there are low initial setup costs and it can be as small or large as the available space.
- Only uses one tank. The main tank houses both the nutritional water and the plants. Some growers use interconnected growing tanks and circulate the water between them. However, this requires a pump.
- Plants sit with their roots suspended in the water via hanging baskets. Alternately, holes can be cut into the lid of the reservoir tank. The plant sits in the lid with their roots suspended in the water through the holes.
- No water pump is required because plants sit in the nutritional water continuously.
- You'll need to top up the tank with water and nutrients will as they are used up by the plants.
- A system of aeration is needed to ensure the plants receive the necessary oxygen.

**WATER CULTURE**

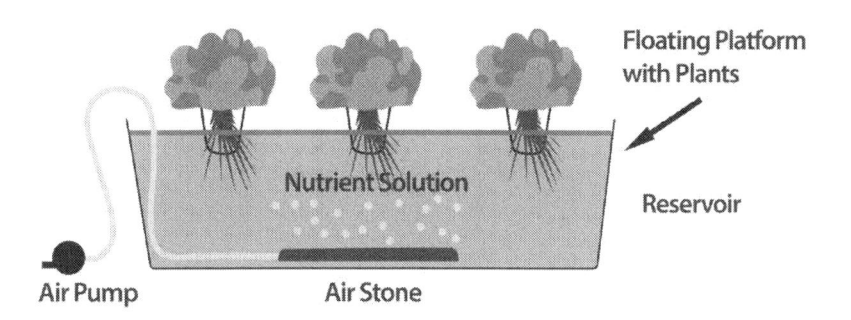

Here are some options you have for oxygenating the water:

- **Air Pump**

Pumps the oxygen into an air stone that sits on the bottom of the tank. Air bubbles rise into the water for the roots.

- **Waterfall**

Water cascades into the tank at force, agitating and aerating the water in the reservoir.

- **Recirculating Water**

Similar to the Ebb and Flow System. The water never completely drains out and the roots are always submerged. Water is pumped into the growing pots, ensuring the plants receive sufficient oxygen to thrive. Once the water reaches a certain level, it is returned to the reservoir via an overflow.

# Aeroponics

This type of system isn't a top choice for home growers even though it works quite well. The set-up can be complicated and the system is very particular. There is not a lot of room for mistakes. This is a system better suited for those experienced with hydroponic cannabis growing.

- Aeroponics is known as vertical farming and is one of the leading hydroponic systems in the commercial industry. It's a great method for any indoor gardener.
- Only one tank is required for aeroponic systems.
- Roots hang down through holes in the lid of the tank. The difference between this system and the water culture method is that the roots are not suspended in water. Instead, they remain exposed to the air. This makes for an oxygen rich atmosphere.
- The plants do not need any growing medium.

- The tank has nutrients and water at the bottom and a pump for water delivery.
- The roots are sprayed by water and nutrients in short bursts from a sprinkler underneath. This requires that the sprinkling system be set up inside the tank.
- The growing tank is the most important element of this system. When set up correctly, it retains humidity and allows for a constant flow of fresh oxygen.
- The tank should be airtight so pests cannot get inside. This will protect the exposed roots.
- If the pump stops for any reason, the roots can dry up quickly and the entire crop will be lost.
- This spray method can be set up in different ways. Each system will alter the size of the droplets in the sprinkling: High Pressure, Low Pressure and Foggers. The higher the pressure, the larger the droplets. The Fogger has the smallest droplets and provides water in the form of a mist.

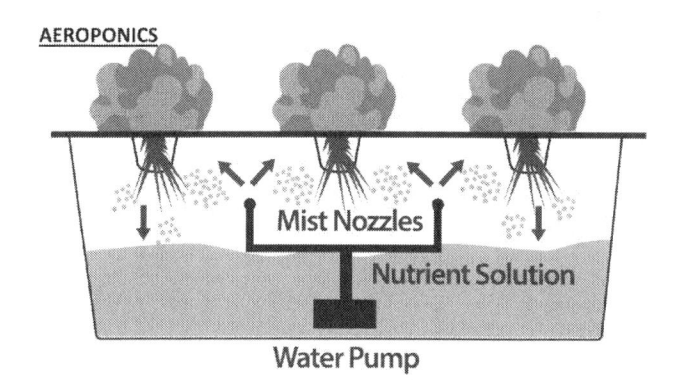

**AEROPONICS**

Mist Nozzles
Nutrient Solution
Water Pump

# Wick Irrigation

This method is not recommended for cannabis growing at all. The wicks do not draw up enough water for the plants to grow and thrive as much as one wants.

- This is the simplest method. It is also the most cost-effective means of growing plants hydroponically.
- Requires no use of pump or electricity.
- Only one tank is needed. The plant containers sit above the reservoir that contains the nutrients and water. A wick(s) hangs down and drops into the water solution. It soaks up the nutritional water, which in turn dampens the plant medium, to feed the roots.
- The system can be as simple as one plant pot that sits above the reservoir. Its wick hangs and enters through a hole. Larger systems could include several plants in a tray with multiple wicks hanging into the solution.
- The growing medium will need flushing periodically to stop algae or mineral build up.

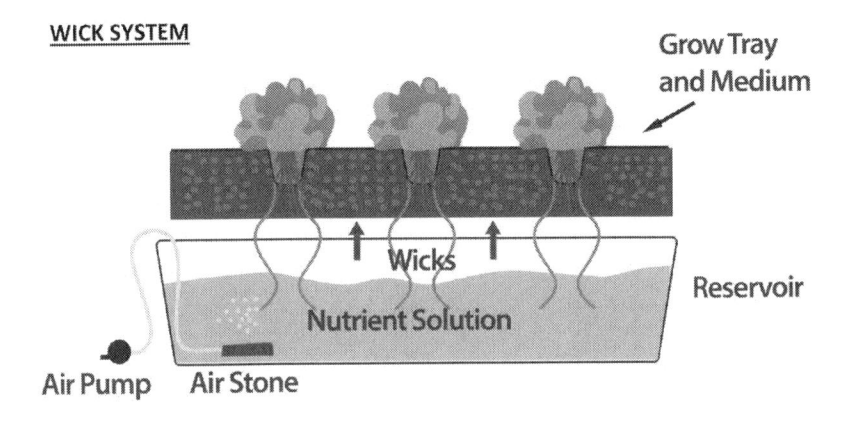

# The Best 3 Hydroponic Systems for Growing Marijuana

|  | Cost | Ease of Use | Yields |
|---|---|---|---|
| **Water Culture** | Low | Easy | Medium |
| **Bubbleponics** | Low | Easy | Medium |
| **Ebb & Flow** | Medium | Medium | High |

## Water Culture

The Water Culture hydroponic method is great for growing cannabis because it's simple to set up, expand, and gives great yields. It's the best system for beginner growers and can be adapted to all types of locations and set-ups. It can be set-up in the smallest of spaces like closets and spare rooms. The ability to expand the system to grow more plants is also a huge benefit. A grower can start off with 2-3 plants and then expand it to many more without a lot of effort. As far as learning hydroponics and getting accustomed to this new way of growing, the Water Culture method is the perfect introduction.

Water Culture systems are easy to set-up, give nice yields, and don't cost much to start. They are easy to assemble and maintain, as well. The downsides are the difficulty in maintaining the appropriate water temperature and keeping the pH and nutrient levels balanced correctly. It's also limiting if you want to grow an especially large quantity of plants.

## Bubbleponics

Bubbleponics is a hybrid variation on the Water Culture Method of hydroponics with the Drip Method. A Bubbleponic system has the roots of the cannabis plants suspended in water while air is bubbled up to them. The bubbles provide the roots with all the fresh oxygen they need and the plants grow fast because of this. In addition, the plants are also fed from the top to maximize growth potential. In a normal WC method, there is no top-feed set-up. This system could be set-up without the top-feed and it would work just fine. However, adding the top-feed greatly increases growth and yields so it is highly recommended and it doesn't take that much more additional effort to do.

Bubbleponics systems produce good yields with a relatively low start-up cost. They are easy to set-up and maintain. The biggest downside to this system is the reliance on the pump, which could fail and kill the crop. We advise always having a second pump on hand in case of failure. That way, you can fix the problem fast and hopefully in time.

## Ebb & Flow

This method isn't the best for the very new beginner to hydroponics. It takes a bit more time commitment to succeed using this method, however, the results and yields are well worth it. The set-up of this system isn't difficult yet does require more time than the other two systems listed. This method is another one that can be done on a small scale and then expanded as needed or necessary. That is the best way to start this hydroponic method because you can try it and see if you like it with just a few plants and then expand if you want to.

This method is favored by many because of its high yields and because once it's set-up, it's easy to use. The downsides to this method are the higher maintenance needs as compared to other methods. The water needs to be replaced more often which also means the nutrients do as well and so it uses more of both, raising costs.

# Ideal Environment for Hydroponic Marijuana

Maintaining an ideal environment is the key to successful hydroponic cannabis growing. During each stage of growth, the marijuana plants will have different needs. Providing the plants with what they need exactly when they need it is crucial to their healthy development. This chapter addresses different nutrient choices, lighting methods, and growing mediums that are vitally important for the health of your plants. The ones that are best for your hydroponic system depend entirely on which system you are using, how much marijuana you are growing, and what options are available where you live.

**What Does Hydroponic Marijuana Need?**

1. Light
2. Water
3. Nutrients
4. Air (temperature and humidity included here)
5. Grow Medium (which can just be nutrient enriched water)

Nutrients are produced by several different commercial companies, and each has pros and cons. Once you understand how to interpret the numbers on the bottle, you'll be much better prepared to decide which is best for your system. Lighting is pretty straight-forward. If your system has access to the sun, then you won't need to consider lighting at all. On the other hand, appropriate lighting is a necessity for indoor growing. There is a huge range of options for growing mediums and it may take some experimenting to find which one works best for your situation.

## A Clean Space

Before we get into nutrients, lights, growing mediums and all the supplies you will need to get your growing started, it's important to make sure the space you are using is clean. This means scrub the floors, the walls, and the grow space to remove any contaminants. Vacuum the corners to remove dust, mold, and bugs that can infiltrate your plants. Wash all your equipment and sterilize it. Unsterilized equipment can pass on pests and diseases from one grow to another and from one plant to another.

## Feeding the Plants

Since hydroponic systems don't use soil, the nutrients added to the water must contain all the minerals plants need to thrive. The selection of the appropriate nutrient solution is one of the most important decisions of your hydroponic plan. Healthy plant growth depends on having the right balance of nutrients. Marijuana plants need a wide variety of elements, vitamins, and amino acids to thrive and prosper.

There are 16 essential elements that plants need. These elements are absorbed by the plant in different ways. Some get transferred to the plant through the roots, while others are taken in through the pores on the leaf. Carbon, Oxygen, and Hydrogen, three of the most necessary, are available in both air and water. These need to be monitored and balanced. One common problem in hydroponics is a lack of sufficient carbon dioxide.

The next big three elements, Nitrogen, Phosphorus, and Potassium, are provided in the fertilizer nutrient blends made for growing hydroponic plants. A fine balance of these is extremely important. This is often referred to as the N-P-K mix.

When looking at bottles or bags of fertilizer, you'll see a list of three numbers on the front, separated by dashes. It will look something like this: 3-4-1. These three numbers refer to the Nitrogen, Phosphorus, and Potassium (N-P-K) proportion of the mix. A 3-4-1 nutrient solution has 30% Nitrogen, 40% Phosphorous, and 10% Potassium.

Calcium, Magnesium, and Sulfur are the next most essential elements. They are also supplied by fertilizer supplements. Calcium is provided through a calcium nitrate (CaNO3) fertilizer. Magnesium and Sulfur are available with magnesium sulfate (MgSO4) supplement.

The remaining 7 essential elements, Copper, Zinc, Boron, Molybdenum, Iron, Manganese, and Chlorine, are rarely deficient. If there is an Iron deficiency, you can supplement your plants with chelated iron.

To make sure your plants get everything they need, specially crafted fertilizer mixes are made for hydroponic crops. These mixes can be added to the water in your reservoir and distributed to your plants through the hydroponic system. Specific fertilizers are created for specific crops and for different stages of growing. There are also nutrient solutions available for soil-based crops. They're not all interchangeable. The hydroponic nutrient mix for tomatoes will be quite different from the one for marijuana. Get the ones that are designed for hydroponic cannabis plants. For example, marijuana nutrient mixes will likely have a higher concentration of phosphorus during the flowering stage because that is one of the main elements needed to develop flavor. Also, get the specialized growing phase mixes. The nutrient mix for the vegetative stage will be quite different from the one for the flowering stage. In the vegetative stage, the plants will need a lot more nitrogen, while in the flowering stage, the nitrogen amount should be cut back to encourage flowering.

## *Types of Nutrient Mixes*

Nutrient mixes are available as liquid or granules. Liquid fertilizer is easy to use. You just pour it into the water reservoir as per bottle instructions. The downside to using liquid fertilizer is that it is more expensive and bulkier to store. Granulated fertilizer is more cost effective, easier to store, and often comes in bulk. However, it isn't as easy to use because it has to be mixed prior to use and it doesn't always dissolve completely. Either one will work fine, so it's a matter of personal preference and what's required by your particular system.

Granulated mixes are available in three types. The one-part mixes are simple and straight-forward. The fertilizer is mixed as indicated on the bag. These are simple to use, but not the best for making stock solutions. Some nutrients in high concentration will form solids. A multi-part solution is better for making stock solutions because the compounds are kept separately. They are relatively easy to mix, too. This is the most common choice for growers who are using granulated nutrient mixes. However, the multi-part mix can be expensive, so it isn't the best choice unless you have a very large garden operation.

Hydroponic fertilizer mixes are also specialized for different stages of growth. They will indicate on the package the stage of growth for which they are designed. Examples of growth stages include vegetative (leaf growth) or blooming (flowering). You'll want to know what you actually want from the plant.

Nutrients are further classified based on the growing medium that is being used. The majority of nutrient mixes are made for a specific growing medium. Pay attention to package specifics and do your homework. If you're using a vermiculite mix but your growing medium is clay pellets, then you won't get optimal results. If the package doesn't give you all the details you need, then a simple online search will lead you in the right direction.

Hydroponic nutrients can be organic or synthetic. Organic fertilizers are best for systems that recirculate or reuse the nutrient solution. These mixes often include materials that can clog up sprayers, drip lines, and pumps. Synthetic nutrients don't have this issue and are therefore more commonly used in hydroponic systems. Organic fertilizers will often have a lower

N-P-K listing than synthetic. However, this doesn't mean they are of lower quality. Synthetic mixes are generally fast-release, as opposed to the slow-release of organic, and so the readily available N-P-K is higher in the synthetic. However, organic mixes will deliver a natural, time release fertilizer that won't burn your roots.

When searching for nutrients, you will encounter a slew of brands and products. While they'll all claim to be the best, there's a great deal of variety in quality from one brand to the next, even among products designed for the same purpose. A brand or company might be good for one thing, but not so great for another.

The best way to deal with this is to read reviews from several growers to find out which products they prefer. This will provide you solid feedback from people who have been there. Find hydroponic forums where you can post the details of your system and crop. You'll get plenty of responses from experienced growers that will direct you to products that have worked for them in similar situations.

## The Essential Elements Needed For Cannabis Plants to Thrive

A macro element is a nutrient that a plant needs in large amounts. A micro element is a nutrient that a plant needs in small amounts.

### Macro Elements

- *Potassium (K)* facilitates the movement of nutrients, water, and sugar in the plant tissue. It is an essential part of early plant growth, protein production, and flower formation.
- *Phosphorous (P)* helps plants transform energy from the sun into chemical energy. It is especially important during the maturation phase of the plant. In marijuana growing, phosphorous impacts the creation of oils,

waxes, terpenes, and plant sugars which give marijuana its' flavor.

- *Nitrogen (N)* is a building material used by proteins and enzymes. It is one of the most important parts of all plants.
- *Sulfur (S)* functions in many ways during plant metabolism and is needed for root growth and seed production.
- *Magnesium (Mg)* is part of the chlorophyll in all plants and is essential for photosynthesis.
- *Calcium (Ca)* gives the plant strength as part of the cell walls. It assists in the transport and retention of other elements.

*Micro Elements*

- Copper (Cu) is responsible for plant growth and provides resistance against disease.
- Zinc (Zn) assists in the creation of chlorophyll. Plant growth will slow without enough chlorophyll.
- Boron (B) is important for the formation of cell walls in the plant. Roots will become swollen or stop growing if there is a deficiency of boron.
- Molybdenum (Mo) helps plant process essential nitrogen nutrients.
- Manganese (Mn) assists during the photosynthesis process. Without it, plants are slow to grow, if they do at all.
- Chlorine (Cl) is important during photosynthesis and keeps the plant growing healthy and strong.
- Iron (Fe) supports the formation of chlorophyll which keeps the leaves green and gives the plant oxygen.

## Non-essential Vitamins and Amino Acids

These are the nutrients that the marijuana plant itself produces. They can be found in pre-mixed nutrient solutions, however, their necessity has not been proven in growing marijuana.

## **Fertilizers**

The nutrient solution is your fertilizer so there is no need for any other type. Classic fertilizers that you would add to soil-based plants are unnecessary.

There are some of the same concerns, though, and things to watch out for so you don't hurt the plants. Be very careful not to add too many nutrients. Sometimes, there is the idea that since the nutrients are feeding the plants, there is no such thing as too much. Possibly, people think that if they give more nutrients, the plants will grow faster. This is not true. It is very harmful to your marijuana plants to be over-fertilized. It can actually kill them.

It is also possible to under-fertilize the plants; however, this isn't nearly as harmful. At most, you'll see slow growth and sad looking plants but it is unlikely they will die. Follow the instructions on the nutrient solution container to make sure you are giving the appropriate amount.

## **Nutrient Needs per Phase**

Each growing stage has its own requirements for nutrients. Remember, when seeing the numbers on a nutrient solution, the first number is the percentage of nitrogen, the second is the percentage of phosphorous, and the third is the percentage of potassium. Each element provides a vital part in the growth of the plant. Nitrogen increases green vegetative growth, phosphorous affects the plant's sugars and impacts the overall flavor of the bud, and potassium moves nutrients throughout the plant in an efficient manner.

### Germination Growth Phase

A half-strength 5-3-4 nutrient solution will give the seeds the little boost they need to germinate.

### Seedling Growth Phase

While the plant is establishing itself, it needs a relatively even boost to grow well. A nutrient solution of 5-3-4 is ideal.

### Vegetative Growth Phase

If the grow room temperature is below 80F (26C), the plants need a larger amount of nitrogen. A 12-6-6 nutrient solution is recommended in this circumstance. If the temperature is above 80F (26C), a higher amount of nitrogen is not necessary. A 20-20-20 nutrient mix solution is good for this.

### Flowering Phase

During the flowering phase, the marijuana plants will need lots of phosphorous. Recommended nutrient solutions for this phase are 2-4-3, 5-20-10, and 15-30-15.

## pH Requirements

pH is the balance of acidity and alkalinity in your water. The nutrients you add to your water will influence the acid/alkaline balance. pH is measured on a scale from 0-14, with 0 being the most acidic and 14 being the most alkaline or basic. pH tests will tell you how well the plants will be able to use the nutrients. Marijuana plants prefer a specific pH balance. The plants won't be able to absorb the needed nutrients if the pH is too high or too low. Measure the pH after you've added the nutrients and then adjust as needed. A good baseline for cannabis plants is to keep it between 5.5 and 6.5.

pH testing devices include paper litmus test strips, liquid test kits, and electronic testing pens. Paper test strips are the cheapest way to go, but they lack accuracy. Litmus strips change color when you dip them in solution. The resultant color reflects the pH. But checking the resulting color against the chart is a bit subjective, so you won't be able to determine the acidity of the solution with any amount of precision. The results can also be skewed if your nutrient solution isn't clear, which is a problem because many nutrient solutions will color the water.

Liquid test kits offer a fair balance of cost and precision. To use a liquid test kit, you take a small sample of solution and place it into a vial which contains a pH-sensitive dye. As with the litmus test, you will compare the resulting color with a chart. This will help you to determine the pH balance of your solution. The color changes are easier to see, and the test is a bit more sensitive than a litmus test, so the liquid test kit is a bit more accurate. However, liquid test kits can also be skewed by the color of your solution (if it's not clear), so they aren't 100% accurate. However, unless your plants are extremely sensitive, liquid test kits are accurate enough.

If your number one consideration is accuracy in pH testing, digital meters are the way to go. They are more expensive, but they will tell you the pH to a tenth, and they won't be skewed by the color of your nutrient solution. To use a digital meter, you just insert the tip of the meter in the solution and it will provide you a digital reading. The one thing you have to watch out for with these meters is calibration. To calibrate them, you must dip them in a pH neutral solution to provide a baseline. This is easier than it sounds, and you can find plenty of information about it online if you need it.

If you need to adjust the pH, phosphoric acid will raise acidity (lower pH) and lemon juice will lower acidity (raise pH). There are also a number of pH adjustment products readily available in hydroponic stores.

## Nutrient Reservoir Upkeep

Water evaporates and it will evaporate from the holding tank as it is used and absorbed by the marijuana plants. When the water level drops, fill a jug with tap water and let it sit for 3 days so the chlorine will evaporate. Some chlorine is ok for plants but many cities and municipalities add chlorine to drinking water in a harmful amount for plants. Use this water to refill the tank. Do not add additional nutrients at this time.

## *Changing the Nutrient Solution*

Once every two weeks, the nutrient solution in your hydroponic system should be changed. This entails discarding the old solution and adding an entirely new mix. The entire system should be cleaned at this time too before adding the new solution. Clean everything with hot water.

## *All Water is Not Equal*

Water quality is of utmost importance in a hydroponic system. Do not underestimate the necessity of good clean water. Distilled or RO (reverse osmosis) water is the best choice. Tap water or city water can have pollutants, chemicals, additives, and any number of things that can potentially have a negative impact on plant growth. This being said, plants use lots of water. If your prime concern is economy, then you'll use what you've got. Just remember that you get out of the plant what you put into it.

## *Equipment To Measure Nutrient Levels*

To ensure you are providing your plants with the correct amount of nutrients, it is recommended that you get a few tools to measure the amounts. These aren't absolutely necessary, yet they are extremely helpful and will give you better control over your plants' growth, leading to a better harvest.

A **PPM Meter** tells you how many Parts Per Million of each element are in your solution. Nutrients like the all-important Nitrogen, Phosphorous, and Potassium will be measured. The optimal PPM levels shift during the different growth phases so there isn't one number to shoot for. In general, somewhere between 900-2800 is good.

**PPM-EC Meter** – This meter measures the electrical conductivity of the water. It isn't a precise measure but will give you a general idea of how much of each element is in your solution.

**PPM-TDS Meter** – A much more precise tool, this meter measures exactly how much of the elements there are in the nutrient solution.

**pH Meter** – Marijuana plants like a pH between 5.5 and 6.5. 6.0 is the absolute ideal. If the pH is too high or too low, it will slow nutrient absorption and therefore slow the growth of the plants. A pH meter is an inexpensive tool to buy that will make a huge difference in the bounty of your harvest. There are pH Up and pH Down solutions that you can add to your water reservoir to adjust the pH.

# Growing Mediums

In nature, plants rely upon soil for stability and nutrients. Since hydroponic systems use no soil, the plants need to be stabilized and obtain nutrients in other ways. This chapter will help you determine which growing medium is best for your system.

## Growing Mediums

As mentioned before, you have many choices when it comes to growing mediums. The ideal medium for your system depends on which hydroponic system you are using and what you are growing. Common growing mediums are rockwool, coco coir, peat moss, clay pellets, perlite, vermiculite, and gravel. Coco coir is preferred by many growers for its' consistent performance and good results. However, any of these types will work.

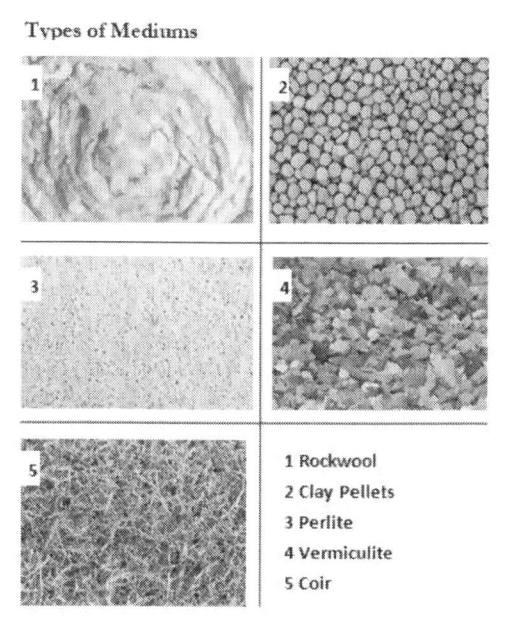

Types of Mediums

1 Rockwool
2 Clay Pellets
3 Perlite
4 Vermiculite
5 Coir

## Rockwool

Rockwool comes in slabs, blocks, and loose fill. It is inorganic, made by melting rocks and spinning them into long, fine fibers. In this sense, it is similar to fiberglass.

Rockwool blocks are great for starting seedlings. In many systems, you don't even have to remove the seedlings from the Rockwool to add them to your system. Simply transfer the entire block and plant to your grow pot.

Rockwool naturally has a high pH level. Because of this, it's necessary to soak it before use. It's also difficult to dispose of properly as the thin fibers won't biodegrade. In essence, they'll last forever.

The high-absorbency of Rockwool makes it a great choice for the Drip System. However, it can become oversaturated. You'll need to monitor the system carefully.

## Coco Coir

Coco coir is made of ground coconut husks. It is quickly becoming a popular choice among hydroponic growers. In nature, coconut husks protect coconuts from sun, sea, and salt damage. When the coconut is ready to sprout, the husk will act as a natural growing medium. By using ground coconut husks in your hydroponic garden, you'll provide these same advantages to your own plants. Coco coir is a renewable, sustainable material. It also looks very much like soil, making it appealing to those who prefer a more natural approach.

Coco coir can hold up to ten times its weight in water. This is great for a hydroponic system. At the same time, it can cause your system to retain too much water. Because of this, Coco Coir is not recommended for constant-flow systems.

Coco coir comes in compressed dry bricks that need to be rehydrated before use. This adds a little extra work to the hydroponic process, but it's not difficult and won't take much time.

If you use coco coir, it's important to choose a nutrient mix specifically designed for this medium. Coco coir binds with iron and magnesium and can starve your plants of these essential elements.

This medium works wonderfully when mixed 50/50 with perlite. Coco Coir retains nutrient solution, while perlite retains oxygen.

## Expanded Clay Pellets

Also referred to as Hydroton, clay pellets are great for many reasons. The clay pellets expand in water to make round, porous balls. Their round shape is stable enough to hold a seedling in place without denying it oxygen or water. These elements can still flow freely around the plant's roots.

One thing to consider is that clay pellets are heavy compared to most mediums. If you fill an entire grow tray with them, you may have a weight issue. Plus, the pellets can dry out quickly because there is so much space between them. If you're not careful, this can cause your roots to dry out, stopping plant growth altogether.

Clay pellets are great for a Drip System because you can run the dripper constantly without worrying about oversaturation or excess dryness.

## Perlite

Perlite is aerated volcanic rock. It is light and porous and has been used for years in both soil and hydroponic gardens. Perlite is excellent for retaining oxygen levels. The downside is it is lightweight. It can easily get washed away or shifted from where you want it. For this reason, it is commonly mixed with another medium, like coco coir or vermiculite.

## Vermiculite

Vermiculite is a mineral that expands when heated and turns into pebbles. It holds water and wicks well, meaning it will draw water and nutrients upwards. The downsides are that it can hold too much water and it is more expensive than most other mediums. If you choose to include vermiculite in your mix, the best option is to blend a small amount of it with other mediums.

## Gravel

Gravel is the cheapest material you can use. If you're on a tight budget, this is the material for you. You'll need to wash it before you use it, so that you can save the sensitive roots of your plants from harmful bacteria or other detrimental substances. Another downside is that it's quite heavy. If you use lots of gravel, you'll need to make sure your system has enough structural stability to handle it.

The table points out some of the main characteristics of each medium.

| Medium | Good Drainage | Water Retention | Oxygen Retention | Good Stability | Can Dry Out |
|---|---|---|---|---|---|
| *Rockwool * Basalt | ✓ | ✓ | ✓ | ✓ | ✓ |
| *River Rock | ✓ | X | ✓ | ✓ | ✓ |
| * Clay Pellets | ✓ | X | ✓ | ✓ | ✓ |
| *Sand | ✓ | X | X | ✓ | ✓ |
| *Coco Coir *Coco chips | ✓ | ✓ | ✓ | ✓ | ✓ |
| *Vermiculite | X | ✓ | X | ✓ | X |
| *Perlite | ✓ | X | ✓ | ✓ | X |

## Starter Plugs/Cubes

Starter plugs are small, compact masses of material used to start seedlings. There is a hole in the top of the plug for the seed to be placed. Once they are watered, seeds will germinate in starter plugs faster than in soil or other materials. They contain all the nutrients that your seeds need to get started. Some starter plugs even come with seeds already in them.

Starter plugs can be made of a number of different materials. The most common materials are Rockwool, peat moss, and pine pulp. If they dry out, it can be hard to rehydrate them, so make sure to keep them sufficiently watered.

The biggest benefit of starter plugs in a hydroponic system is that the seedlings don't need to be transplanted. They can be placed directly into your system without being removed from the plug.

**Growing Medium Notes**

Please notice I do not include peat moss in this list. Even though it has been commonly used in hydroponic systems, it is not a renewable resource. If you'd like to learn more about this, do a little digging. There's plenty of available information which explains in-depth the environmental impact of extensive peat moss use.

# Lighting

Marijuana plants need about 20 hours of light during the vegetative stage and around twelve hours of light per day during the flowering stage. Remember that plants get their energy from light. If your hydroponic system isn't in a place where it is getting natural light from the sun, you'll need to set up a lighting system.

Plants have rhythms, just like we do. The optimal light schedule will differ depending on the growth stage of the plant as well. Marijuana plants grow well vegetatively when provided with constant light, but need cycles of light and darkness to trigger flowering.

If you don't want to be bothered with lighting systems, there is also the option of growing auto-flowering cannabis seeds. These plants go through their entire life cycle in around 3 months regardless of the light provided them. Of course, providing correct lighting will give you better harvests even with auto-flowering plants; however, you don't have to bother with the lighting set-ups if you don't want to.

The type of lighting you need depends on a wide variety of factors specific to your system: enclosure type, plant type, system size, ventilation, and last but not least, budget. Fluorescent tubes are good for a single low-budget system. Small systems will fare better with CFLs (Compact Fluorescent Lamps). These lights were designed as an efficient alternative to incandescent bulbs. They screw into a standard socket and provide sufficient light, but you may want to arrange reflectors so that the light is focused on the plant.

HIDs (High-Intensity Discharge lamps) are another option. They are a bit more costly than CFLs, but they are a preferred lighting option for experienced growers. This is because they have a very high light output and are from four to eight times more efficient than standard incandescent bulbs. However, they produce a lot of heat, so you'll have to ventilate your system to prevent it from drying out.

Another option is to use LEDs (Light Emitting Diode lamps). This is the high-tech option and will cost quite a bit more at the beginning, but they use a fraction of the electricity of other options and produce less heat. LEDs can also be calibrated to produce the exact spectrum of light that your plant needs. If you only plan to grow one crop, it's probably not worth it to purchase LEDs. But, if this is the beginning of a long relationship with hydroponic growing, they will more than pay off in the long run.

## Fluorescent Lights

Fluorescent lights are available in a wide range of sizes and spectrums. They are not ideal for large plants but they will work. They are generally inexpensive, easy to set up, and will work in a pinch.

## Compact Fluorescent Light Bulbs (CFL)

These are a good choice because they aren't too expensive and they don't require any special wiring or set-up (they screw into a regular light socket). They produce light in all directions and are best used with a reflector so you don't waste any heat or light.

High output (HO) T5 fluorescent grow lights are the best ones to get if you are going to purchase compact fluorescent lights. They do not require any special set-up like ballasts or reflectors. Nor do they need a cooling system. It takes about 19 4-foot long T5 HO bulbs to match the output of one 600 watt HPS bulb. Space can be an issue using these since it can take a lot to generate the light you need.

## High-Intensity Discharge (HID) Lights

HID lights have a high light output and are a preferred choice for growers. Using HIDs will be better for your plants than fluorescent and less expensive than incandescent bulbs in the long run. At the same time, they are expensive, require a special set-up, and need ventilation because of their high heat output.

There are two types of HID lights:

- **Metal Halide (MH) lights**, which give off a blue-white light that is ideal for vegetative growth.
- **High-Pressure Sodium (HPS) lights**, which give off an orange-red light that is ideal for flowering.

In a perfect set-up, you would have both these types of HID lights and switch them out as needed. If you can only choose one, however, choose the HPS because it gives out more light per watt and the flowering stage is much more sensitive than the vegetative.

HID lights require a ballast and hood/reflector for each light. There are some newer ballasts that will run both MH and HPS lights. Many, though, are designed for one or the other which means you will have to buy the correct ballast for each one which can get expensive.

Ballasts can be magnetic or digital. Magnetic ones are less expensive but they are less efficient and run hotter. Digital ballasts are more efficient and also more expensive.

In addition to ballasts, the lamps will need to be mounted on air-cooled reflector hoods since they produce a lot of heat. This will necessitate the need exhaust fans and ducting which can be quite expensive.

## LED Lights

LED lights can provide the exact spectrum of light your plant needs. They last longer than all other lights and use less electricity. The upfront cost, however, is imposing. As mentioned above, LEDs are worth it if you plan to be growing many crops over the years. For a once-off, though, you may be better off with a different option.

## Which Light Type is Best?

The timing of light cycles and the types of light are extremely important to the success of marijuana plants. And, it isn't the same through the entire growth process. The vegetative and flowering stages have different light needs. And, because of this, you may want to consider having several different types of lights so you can provide them with what they need at the right moment. There isn't really a one-lamp-fits-all situation here.

The early growing phases of marijuana plants like high amounts of blue wavelength light, around 14%, which promote bushy, compact plants. An MH lamp gives off the most amount of this light.

In the bud formation and flowering stages, marijuana plants like more orange and red wavelength light and only a small amount of blue light. The HPS lamps provide the best orange and red light.

An HPS lamp can be used for the entire grow cycle but the plants will be taller and not as bushy since they aren't getting the preferred amounts of blue wavelength light. HPS lights only give out around 2-6% blue light. CFL lights are added by many growers in addition to the HPS lamps just during the vegetative stage. The CFL lights will add the necessary blue light and since they don't produce as much heat, they can be placed closer to the plants.

The more expensive LED lights, on the other hand, provide all the light needs of the marijuana plant from seed to bud. In addition, they use 50% less electricity than HPS lights. The investment is definitely something to consider.

# Using Lights to Grow

The grow cycle of the marijuana plant can be controlled by you through the light you give it. A plant can be kept in the vegetative state indefinitely as long as it only gets 6 hours of darkness. Simply put, you can trigger the growing stages by adjusting the amount and type of light it receives on a daily basis.

In a natural environment, marijuana plants will start to grow in the spring when it isn't too hot out. The plants move into the vegetative state directly after germination. At the end of the summer, they will begin to flower as the days grow shorter. To replicate this in a controlled environment, all it takes is some adjustment of the lighting.

When setting up your grow space, it is important to measure how much heat the lights are giving off. A good way to test is to hold your hands at the tops of the plants. If the heat is too much for your hands, it is too much for your plants. Move the lights further away.

### *Lighting for the Vegetative Stage*

The vegetative stage is triggered by keeping the lights on for long periods of time. The lights should be kept on for 18-20 hours and then off for 4-6 hours, leaving the plants in darkness for that short time. The lights to use during this time are the MH lights or LED lights. The HPS lights aren't much use during this time since they don't give off much blue light.

The MH lights give off a lot of heat, though, which can be harsh and detrimental to the plants while they are still young so be careful and monitor your plants frequently to ensure they are ok.

## *Lighting for the Flowering Stage*

Flowering happens in nature when the days begin to shorten at the end of summer. To make this happen in your hydroponic set-up, change the amount of time the plants receive light. They need 12 hours of light and 12 hours of darkness at this point.

Do not trigger the flowering stage until the plants are between 12-20 inches tall. Doing it too early will impact the harvest negatively.

In 1-2 weeks, you will notice the plants changing. If you see any male plants, remove them immediately. Male plants don't produce bud so you definitely don't want them there. In fact, they only produce pollen, which then causes seeds in the female plants and then you end up with seedy weed. Not good!

# Air, Temperature, and Humidity

## Air

All plants need air to survive and marijuana plants are no different. Carbon dioxide (CO2) is vital to the photosynthesis process. The grow room will need a steady supply of fresh air flowing through it.

An exhaust fan will assist in removing warmer air and an air inlet on the opposite side of the room will bring in fresh air. The type of lights you use will greatly impact what size exhaust fan you will need. The HID lights put out a lot of heat and so those set-ups will need larger fans.

We recommend testing the needs of your space before settling any plants in there. Turn on your lights for a while and monitor the temperature for a few days. This will give you a good baseline of how much heat the lights are producing and how much airflow you need to incorporate.

To keep the smell of marijuana plants in full bloom to a minimum, use a charcoal filter with your exhaust fan.

A light constant breeze in the grow room will strengthen the stems of your plants and discourage pests and molds from taking hold. A simple wall mounted circulating fan does this well. Do not direct the fans directly at your plants since that will cause windburn.

## Temperature

The ideal temperature for cannabis plants is between 70F-85F (21-29C) while the lights are on (daytime) and between 58F-70F (14-21C) while the lights are off (nighttime). Different strains will have different preferences so make sure you learn what is best for the seeds you are planting. In general, indica strains prefer temperatures on the lower side of the range.

## Humidity

The humidity requirement of cannabis plants changes depending on the stage they are in. During the seedling stage, the plants like a high humidity level, between 65-70%. The high humidity lets the plants take in water through their leaves which is ideal since their roots are still developing and can't take in much.

The humidity during the vegetative stage can be lower but should be done slowly. Lowering it by 5% each week is good. The range should stay between 40-70%. During the flowering stage, the humidity needs to be between 40-50%. Anything above 60% will not be good for your plants. During the last couple of weeks of flowering, the humidity level needs to range between 30-40%.

## Temperature & Humidity Requirements by Growth Stage

|  | Germination | Seedling | Vegetative | Flowering | Late Flowering |
|---|---|---|---|---|---|
| **Temperature** | 70F-85F 21-29C | 70F-85F 21-29C | 70F-85F 21-29C | 65F-80F 18-26C | 65F-80F 18-26C |
| **Humidity** | 65-70% | 65-70% | 40-70% | 40-50% | 30-40% |

# Equipment for Controlling the Grow Environment

There are a few inexpensive tools that will help greatly in the success of your growing operation. They aren't absolutely necessary, however, without them, you will be doing a lot more work. These are here to make your life easier and to streamline your growing.

## *Timer*

Regardless of which hydroponic set-up you decide on, you will need a device to control the lights. The alternative is turning them on and off yourself every day. That is a huge pain! The range of light control timers goes from very inexpensive to super sophisticated and cost prohibitive.

A simple 24-hour timer is sufficient for a basic growing situation. Your plants will benefit from having a consistent schedule and you will benefit from not having to stress about it all the time.

## *Adjustable Thermostat Switch*

This device plugs into your exhaust fan. You set the desired temperature on the device and the fan will turn on and off automatically to keep that temperature. Not only does this device save money, but it also keeps the necessary steady temperature for your plants. It is far more efficient than you going in to check the temperature several times a day and manually adjusting it!

### *Hygrometer/Thermostat*

These devices are inexpensive and invaluable. They measure the humidity and temperature in the room. If you get one with a high/low memory feature, they will save the highest and lowest readings for the period of time since you last checked. It's a great way to keep tabs on your grow room without having to manually check it every few hours. Plus, it will provide you with valuable statistics as to the environment in the room.

### *Reflectors*

To get the most out of your lights, place reflective material on the walls. Light will bounce off the walls and around the room and will touch every part of your plants.

### *Grow Tent*

The best way to keep light, heat, and humidity in an enclosed space is with a grow tent. There are many available online for decent prices, under $100. The tent should be airtight and water-sealed.

# Hydroponic System Set-Up

## Ready-made Kits vs. DIY

There are many options when it comes to setting up a hydroponic system for growing cannabis. Not only are there different hydroponic growing systems to consider, but there is also the decision as to whether you want to build your own or use a ready-made one. There are a lot of ready-made hydroponic kits on the market and especially for a first-time grower, they are the easier way to go.

Ready-made kits include all the bits and pieces that you need to set up your system, from the reservoir to the drip line to the pumps to the germination cubes. It's an all-in-one system and all you have to do is provide the seeds. They should come with a warranty and customer service too, so if you have any problems, you can return it or get assistance. There are many systems that you can expand as desired, too, which is nice. So, you could start out with a one-plant system and then buy components to add to your system as you desire. Ready-made kits take all the guesswork away and streamline the process. Rarely are they adaptable in the sense that you can't make them do anything else than exactly what they were designed to do.

Buying a ready-made kit reduces a lot of headaches, uncertainties, and is really great for beginners and the DIY-challenged. Of course, this comes at a cost. A real cost – they are a lot more expensive than if you built a system yourself. A ready-made Water Culture bucket system can run anywhere from $40 for one bucket (one plant) to $150+ for 4 buckets (4 plants). An Ebb & Flow ready-made hydroponic kit can cost $250+.

Setting up your own system will take more time, without a doubt. It may require some basic knowledge of tools, including power tools. The biggest upside to building your own hydroponic system is that you can customize it to your specific space and design it to how you want. For example, if you want a system with 10 grow pots, then you can have it even if such an option isn't available to buy. A DIY hydroponic system usually costs much less than a ready-made kit, although that isn't always the case as any experienced DIYer knows. Purchasing the wrong items, finding out certain parts don't fit as expected, this can all add money and time to the project.

If you are a beginner to hydroponics, starting off with a kit is a good way to get a feel as to whether you even like this method of growing. In the end, it really depends on what type of person you are. Do you like to build things on your own or do you prefer to have it all set-up and ready to go without that additional work and potential headache?

Even if you buy a ready-made kit, there will still be costs for fans, humidifiers, air-conditioning, heating, and the like. Don't forget about all that. These costs you will have regardless of which option you choose.

# Set-Up Instruction #1: Water Culture System

## The Five-Gallon Bucket System

This is one of the simplest and best-producing ways of growing cannabis hydroponically. It can be just one plant or a dozen. These instructions are for 1 plant but I think you will see how easily it can be adapted for more. The Water Culture hydroponic system can be set up in a wide variety of ways and this is just one example. This particular way is favored by many because it doesn't cost much to set up at all and the basics of operating it are very easy. And, when you decide to grow more plants, the system is ready to adapt to your needs.

There are pumps that you can attach and run multiple air stones from. This means you can run tubing from the pump to several five-gallon buckets and not worry about having to plug in multiples of pumps.

## *What You Will Need*

- Five-gallon bucket with lid
- 1 Growing container with tapered sides and holes cut in it for roots to grow through
- Air pump
- Air stone
- 3/16" (internal) diameter tubing [or whichever size will fit your air pump]
- Growing medium
- Nutrients
- Cannabis seeds
- Starter cubes for germination
- Lights
- Timer for lights
- 5 gallons water (to start)

# Step By Step Instructions

## *Step #1 – Set Up*

1. Set up the lights, fans, and all else in your grow space that you need.
2. *Assembly:* Cut a hole in the lid of your 5-gallon bucket to fit the growing container. Make sure the hole is smaller than the container so it doesn't fall through. The container should be hanging 2/3rds into the bucket and have 1/3 above the lid. [The goal is to have the plant's roots submerged while being careful not to submerge any part of the plant stem.]

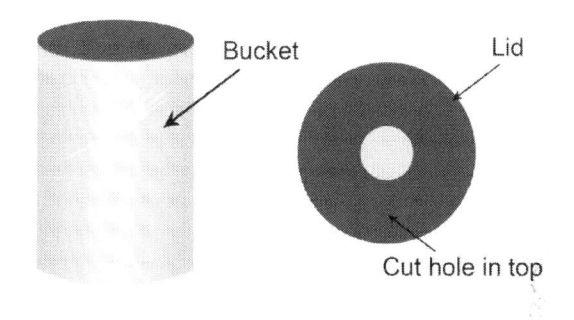

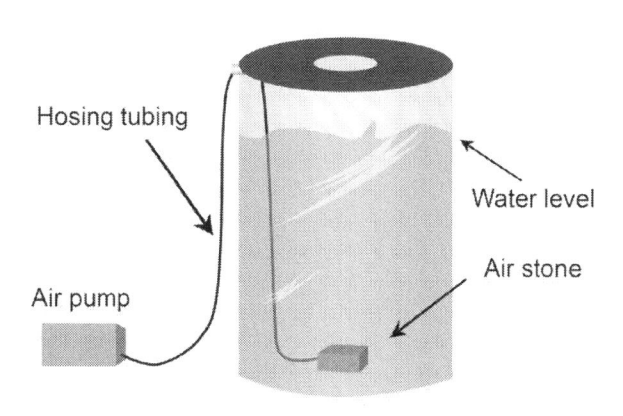

3. Add growing medium to the pot. If the medium begins to fall out of the holes, you can put a small piece of cloth over the holes first. Set aside.
4. Fill the bucket with water. You can always add more later, if needed or remove some.
5. Mix your nutrients per the instructions of the package and add to the water.
6. Test your pH and adjust the nutrients accordingly.
7. Attach the tubing to the air stone and submerge the air stone in the water.
8. Attach the free end of the tubing to the air pump (the air pump DOES NOT go in the water) and arrange it on the side of the bucket.
9. Plug the pump in and verify the air stone is producing bubbles.
10. Secure the lid on top of the bucket.

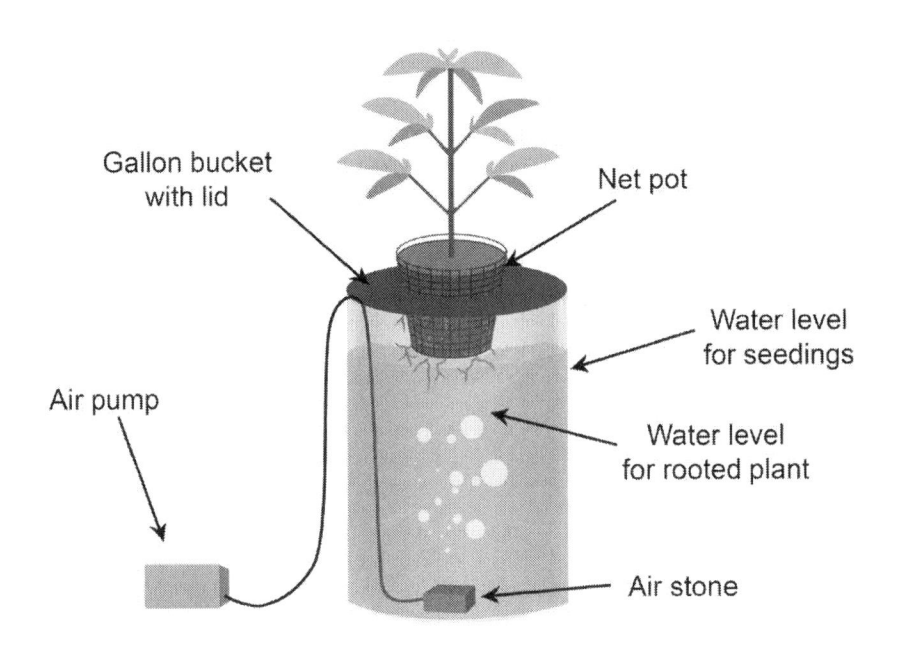

11. Put each seed in its own germination starter cube, about 1/2" deep.
12. Put each germination starter cube with seed in a growing container, snuggling it down a little bit into the grow medium.
13. Pour water very carefully over the germination cubes so they are wet without being drenched.
14. Turn on the air pump.
15. Make sure everything is set up as it should be. The lights should be attached to your timer – make sure it is working right.
16. DO NOT turn on the lights. For the first few days, the seeds need to be in the dark to germinate.

## *Step #2– Germination*

1. Check the plants daily! Check the set-up. Make sure the germination cubes are staying wet and that the pump is working correctly.
2. Maintain a pH between 5.5 and 6.3.
3. Do not turn on the lights until the seedlings burst from the surface of the germination cube.
4. Check water levels. Refill as needed until scheduled time to change it out completely.

## *Step #3 – Seedling*

1. Set light timer for an 18/24 light schedule.
2. Use blue-wavelength lights during this stage. [see lighting information]
3. Continue to check connections, pH levels, light, humidity, and equipment.
4. If the seedling leaves start to yellow or turn brown, cut back the amount of nutrients you are giving them. Drain and replace the water if this is an issue. Alternately, if

the leaves are pale but the pH is correct, increase the amount of nutrients.

5. The plants will be in this stage for 2-3 weeks until they start growing bigger leaves. [see cannabis plant growing stages for more details]
6. Change the nutrient-enriched water every 7 days.
7. Check water levels. Refill as needed until scheduled time to change it out completely.
8. Keep the temperature around 75 degrees for the rest of the growing time. Bacteria can flourish in water reservoirs and high temperatures will encourage the bacteria to grow. There are beneficial bacteria products on the market that can be used to get rid of the bad stuff and introduce good ones.

## *Step #4 – Vegetative Stage*

The amount of time the plants need in this stage will depend on the type and strain of the plants. There is no clear-cut time-period. In general, it is around 2-3 weeks.

1. Keep the light schedule at 18/24.
2. Keep the blue-wavelength lights.
3. As the plants grow, you may need to adjust your lights and move them higher up so they aren't too close to the leaves and burning them.
4. Change the nutrient-enriched water every 7 days being mindful of any changes in leaf color and reducing/increasing nutrient levels as needed.
5. The plants are growing rapidly at this point and therefore using more water. Check water levels more frequently to make sure they have enough. Refill as needed.
6. Check the pH regularly.

7. Check the water for bacteria growth, cloudiness, and smells. Check the roots for root rot.
8. Monitor equipment.

## *Step #5 – Flowering Stage*

As with the vegetative stage, the amount of time a plant will flower before being ready to harvest is dependent on variety and strain. This stage is the longest and will last from 4-12 weeks.

1. Change the light schedule to 12/12.
2. Switch to an orange-red wavelength lighting system.
3. Check water levels. Refill as needed until scheduled time to change it out completely.
4. Change the nutrient-enriched water every 7 days or as needed. Switch to a flowering nutrient formula for this stage.
5. Check the pH regularly.
6. Check the roots of your plants for any color changes – white are great, brown or slimy is bad.
7. Investigate for male/female/hermaphrodite plants! Remove any that aren't female.

## *Step #6 – Harvest*

1. Refer to the harvesting section to know the appropriate time to harvest.

# Set-Up Instruction #2: Bubbleponics

## The 10-Gallon Tote Container System

This guide is to set up one reservoir which will grow 1-2 plants. You will be planting four and then selecting the two strongest. It is tempting to grow them all once they start; however, they will end up crowded and won't grow well this way. Keep it to 1-2 per reservoir! If all 4 take off, you can set up another reservoir once they get to the vegetative state and move the extra ones over to it. You can set up as many reservoirs as you like or as you have space to put in. In this method, since the plants grow so quickly, it's important to keep a close eye on them. If they are allowed to stay in the vegetative state too long, they will grow wild and take up all your space. It's best to make sure there is space around each plant and to get them flowering as soon as possible to control the vegetative growth. This method can be adapted to fit the previous instructions for the Water Culture single bucket system. To adapt it, you would need to lay out drip lines to each bucket from the main reservoir.

### *What You Will Need*

- Lights (CFLs are an easy and inexpensive way to go)
- Nutrients
- 10-gallon plastic tote container with a lid
- Table that can hold heavy 10-gallon tote container
- 5 Net pots
- Water pump

- 4-port Drip irrigation manifold for 1/2" tubing (female pipe thread)
- Air pump
- 3/16" (internal) diameter tubing [or whichever size will fit your air and water pumps]
- 1/2" (internal) diameter tubing [or whichever size will fit your water pump and manifold]
- 2 large air stones (one will be ok too)
- 24-hour timer
- Hydroton rocks or other grow medium
- Twist ties or gardening tape
- 4 cannabis seeds
- 5 gallons water (to start)
- Clay pellets (grow medium)
- 4 Germination starter cubes

## Step By Step Instructions

### Step #1 – Set Up

1. Building the reservoir:

    a) Cut out 5 holes in the lid of the 10-gallon tote container. Use the net pot to space and trace them out evenly on the surface before cutting. The holes should be slightly smaller than the net pots since you want them to rest easily in there without slipping right through into the water.

    b) Arrange the holes so it looks like the number "5" on a dice. 2 holes on one end, one in the middle, and two more holes on the other end.

    c) There are many ways to cut holes – a power drill or hole saw, scissors, box cutter – whichever method you use, be careful! Cutting hard plastic can be tricky as the knife can easily slip.

d) Make two notches in the top lip of the container to run the water pump cord and tubes through. Put the notches opposite each other on the shorter sides of the container.

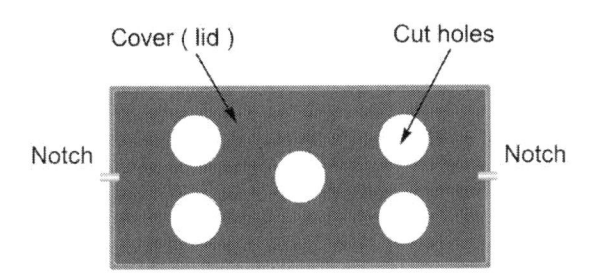

2. Soak the air stone(s) in water.
3. Set up your lights.
4. Set up and arrange the table underneath your lights.
5. Rinse the clay pellets until the water runs clear. Set aside.
6. Place the reservoir container on top of your table.

7. Place the air pump next to the container in a secure place.
8. Put the air stones at the bottom of the reservoir.
9. Attach the 3/16" tubing to the air stones and run the tubing outside the reservoir to reach the air pump and cut the pieces so they fit. Use the notches to hold the tubing. [do not plug in air pump yet!]

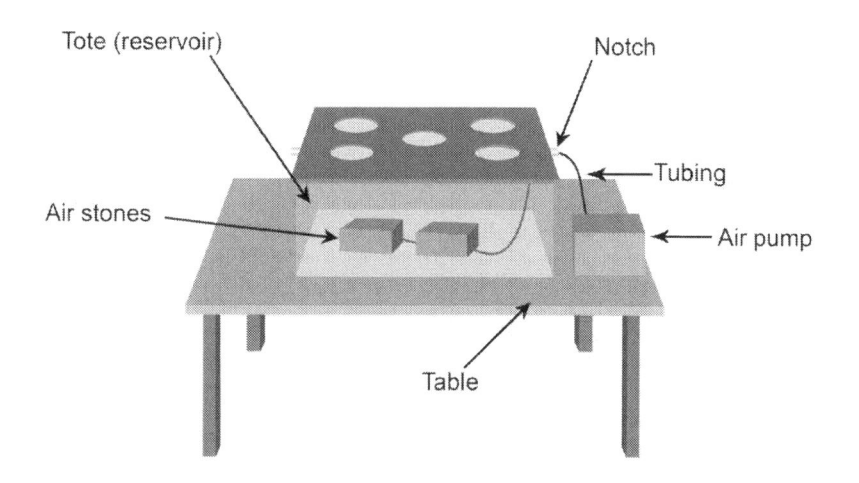

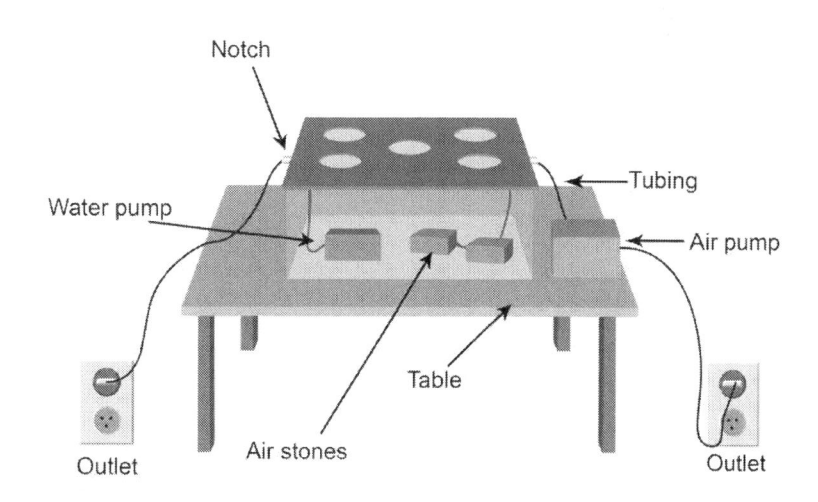

10. Put the water pump inside the reservoir and run the power cord outside the reservoir through the notches.
11. Cut a 5" piece of the 1/2" tubing and use it to connect the top of the water pump with the bottom of the drip manifold.
12. Cut 4 1 1/2" pieces of the 3/16" tubing and attach them to the ports of the drip manifold.
13. Turn on the valve of each port that you have a tube connected to.

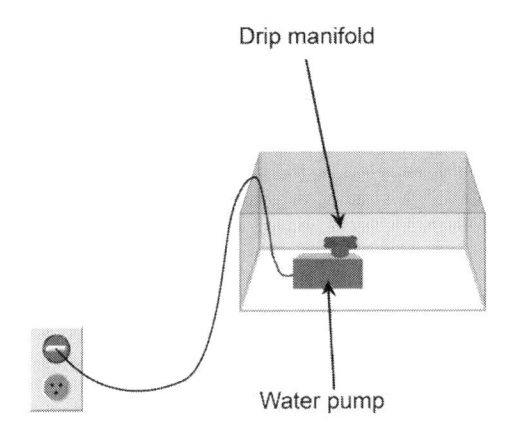

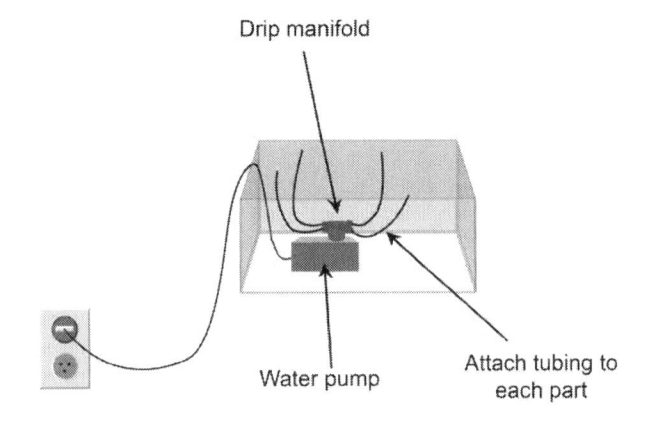

14. Place the net pots in the slots in the lid leaving the middle one open. This is where you will add water, check water levels, and check connections.
15. This is a tricky bit – take your time! Using the hole in the middle, reach into the reservoir and take each piece of tubing from the drip manifold and lead them, one each, to the net pots. There should be one line going into each net pot. Put the tube through the gaps in the net pot to secure it.

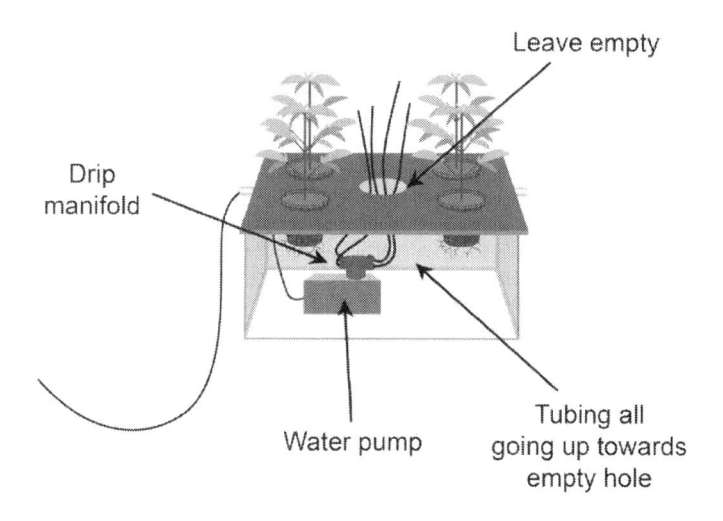

Leave empty

Drip manifold

Water pump

Tubing all going up towards empty hole

16. Mix the Nutrients (start with ½ recommended dosage and increase incrementally). Pour the 5 gallons of nutrient-enriched water into the reservoir, being careful not to disturb tubing.
17. Fill the net pots with 1" of the rinsed clay pellets, again, being careful not to dislodge the tubing into the pots.
18. Put each seed in its' own germination starter cube, about 1/2" deep.
19. Put each germination starter cube with seed on top of one of the clay pellet lined net pots.

20. Rearrange the tubes going into the net pots as needed so that they are almost touching the germination cubes.
21. Fill the net pots up with more clay pellets until they are even with the height of the germination cube.
22. Fill the remaining net pot with clay pellets and set it in the middle hole. This hole is your access point but it can't be left open since it will allow light to infiltrate and cause root rot or other problems.
23. Pour water very carefully over the germination cubes so they are wet without being drenched.
24. Turn on your pumps.

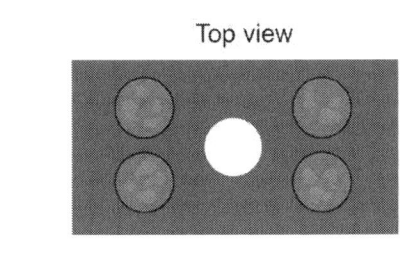

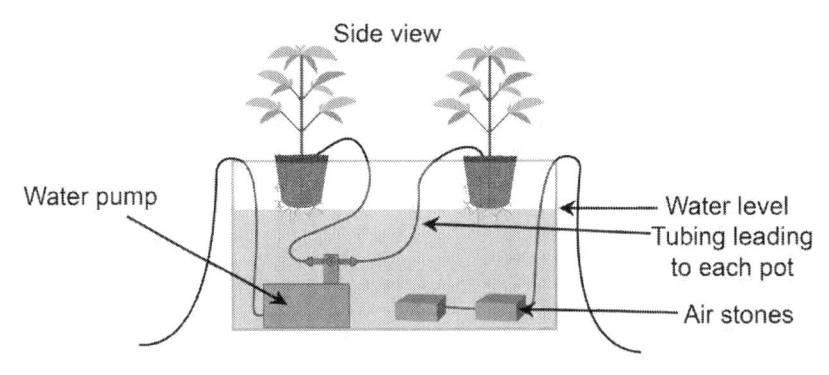

25. Make sure everything is set up as it should be. The lights should be attached to your timer – make sure it is working right. Everything else (air pump, water pump, etc...) are running 24 hrs/day and do not need a timer.
26. DO NOT turn on the lights. For the first few days they seeds need to be in the dark to germinate.

## *Step #2 – Germination*

1. Check the plants daily! Check the set-up. Make sure the germination cubes are staying wet and that the pumps are working correctly. Most of all check that the tubing going into each net pot is still secure.
2. Maintain a pH between 5.5 and 6.3.
3. Do not turn on the lights until the seedlings burst from the surface of the germination cube.

## *Step #3 – Seedling*

1. Set light timer for an 18/24 light schedule.
2. Use blue-wavelength lights during this stage. [see lighting information]
3. Continue to check connections, pH levels, light, humidity, and equipment.
4. If the seedling leaves start to yellow or turn brown, cut back the amount of nutrients you are giving them. Drain and replace the water if this is an issue. Alternately, if the leaves are pale but the pH is correct, increase the amount of nutrients.
5. The plants will be in this stage for 2-3 weeks until they start growing bigger leaves. [see cannabis plant growing stages for more details]
6. Change the nutrient-enriched water every 7 days.
7. Keep the temperature around 75 degrees for the rest of the growing time. Bacteria can flourish in water reservoirs and high temperatures will encourage the bacteria to grow. There are beneficial bacteria products on the market that can be used to get rid of the bad stuff and introduce good ones.
8. It is at the end of this stage that you can choose the two best growing plants and discard the others. Or, build another reservoir and move two plants over to that one

so each reservoir only has 2 plants in it and all of them have room to grow.

## *Step #4 – Vegetative Stage*

The amount of time the plants need in this stage will depend on the type and strain of the plants. There is no clear-cut time-period. In general, it is around 2-3 weeks.

1. Keep the light schedule at 18/24.
2. Keep the blue-wavelength lights.
3. As the plants grow, you may need to adjust your lights and move them higher up so they aren't too close to the leaves and burning them.
4. Change the nutrient-enriched water every 7 days being mindful of any changes in leaf color and reducing/increasing nutrient levels as needed.
5. The plants are growing rapidly at this point and therefore using more water. Check water levels more frequently to make sure they have enough. Refill as needed.
6. Check the pH regularly.
7. Check the water for bacteria growth, cloudiness, and smells. Check the roots for root rot.
8. Monitor equipment.

## *Step #5 – Flowering Stage*

As with the vegetative stage, the amount of time a plant will flower before being ready to harvest is dependent on variety and strain. This stage is the longest and will last from 4-12 weeks.

1. Change the light schedule to 12/12.
2. Switch to an orange-red wavelength lighting system.

3. Change the nutrient-enriched water every 7 days or as needed. Switch to a flowering nutrient formula for this stage.
4. Check the pH regularly.
5. Check the roots of your plants for any color changes – white is great, brown or slimy is bad.
6. Investigate for male/female/hermaphrodite plants! Remove any that aren't female.

## *Step #6 – Harvest*

1. Refer to the harvesting section to know the appropriate time to harvest.

**TIP**

- Have an extra batch of nutrient-enriched water on hand. Use it to top off your reservoir.
- Change entire reservoir every 7 days (do not let roots dry out!)
- A battery powered water transfer pump makes quick work of the draining process.
- An electric water transfer pump is also an option but costs more
- Use a siphon or if the reservoir is off the ground, you can just drain it.

# Set-Up Instruction #3: Ebb and Flow System

This set-up is to create a system of containers that can grow 3-4 cannabis plants (depending on the type and anticipated size of final plants). The system can be adapted and added to in order to grow more plants. You can also set up several ebb and flow systems separate from each other. This set-up is inexpensive to build which makes it ideal as a starter system. It does require some basic knowledge of using power tools but nothing too fancy. It is of utmost importance that the surface you are setting the grow tray on is level. Water will pool in the tray if the surface isn't level and cause root rot.

In these instructions, I've listed specific sizes for the grow tray and reservoir bins but this is actually more of a suggestion. A grow tray can be of any size. It can be large or small to accommodate your space availability or based on how many plants you'd like to grow. If you have an especially large table, you could get a larger grow tray. Just make sure you aren't crowding the cannabis plants – they need space to spread out.

Additionally, the size of the reservoir depends on how many plants you are growing because you need to make sure there is enough water to flood your grow tray. Reservoir size is also dependent on how much space you have. The smaller your reservoir, the more often you will have to replenish the nutrient-water solution. Don't forget, the larger the plants grow (and they can get big!), the more nutrition they will need. While they are first growing, they won't be using as much, yet as the weeks go on, you may wish you'd gone with a bigger reservoir. If you have the space for it, use a large reservoir.

An opaque reservoir container is recommended. With this, you can easily see how full it is and therefore know when you need to add water and at the same time not have to worry about too much light getting in. If you get a transparent container, you will be able to see water levels but you will also need to cover the sides somehow so the light doesn't encourage algae growth. A removable covering is best in these situations.

Please see the notes at the end regarding mediums, timers, fill & drain fittings, and tubing.

## *What You Will Need*

- 30-40 gallon storage tote bin with lid, preferably opaque or dark colored for the reservoir
- 40+ quart clear storage tote bin for the grow tray
- Sturdy level table that can hold the weight of the grow tray bin + weight of full-grown plants
- Timer
- Clay pebbles (or other growing medium)
- 2-3 large containers for plants (or more) --- containers must have holes in the bottom so nutrient water can flow through.
- Irrigation tubing, 1/2" inner diameter
- Submersible pond pump with 1/2" fittings
- Fill and drain fitting set, 1/2"
- Power drill with appropriate fittings to drill holes in plastic for fill and drain fitting set and for overflow tubing.
- Nutrients
- Marijuana seeds

# Step By Step Instructions

## *Step #1 – Set Up*

1. Set up your lighting system & fans.

2. *Building the System:* Place the grow tray tote bin on top of the table. Allow a small part of the bin to overhang over the edge of the table so you can run your inlet and outlet drains between the grow tray on top of the table to the reservoir which will be under the table.

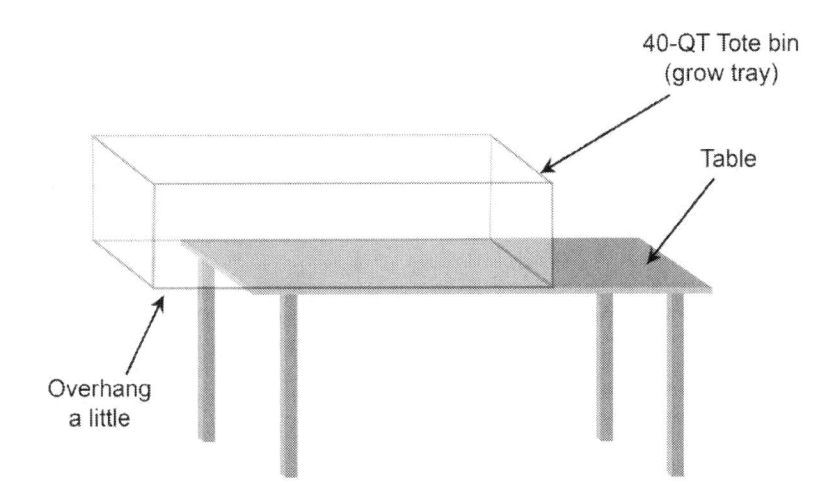

40-QT Tote bin (grow tray)

Table

Overhang a little

3. Drill two holes in the bottom of the smaller container where it overhangs over the table edge. These are for your inlet (water going into grow tray) and overflow (water draining out). The inlet hole will need to accommodate your fill fitting so measure accordingly. The overflow hole is where the tubing goes, so make it a little bit smaller than your tubing so it can fit securely. If you make it too big, you will need to get wider tubing.

**Drill holes**

**Table**

**Drill holes for tubing**

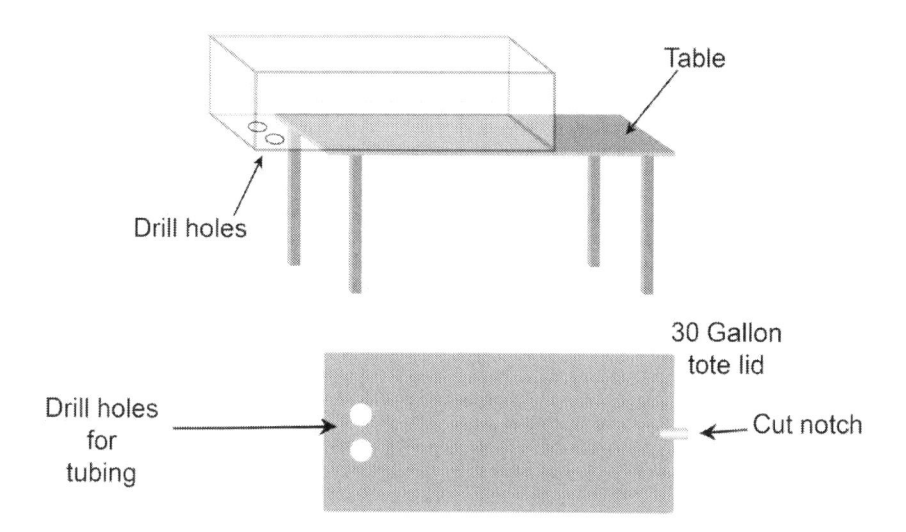

**30 Gallon tote lid**

**Cut notch**

4. Drill two holes in the lid of the reservoir. Both will have tubing fed through them – one to attach the pump and inlet fitting and the other for the overflow tubing.
5. Cut a small notch in the lip of the lid of the reservoir container for the pumps power cord to go through.
6. Place the reservoir underneath the table.

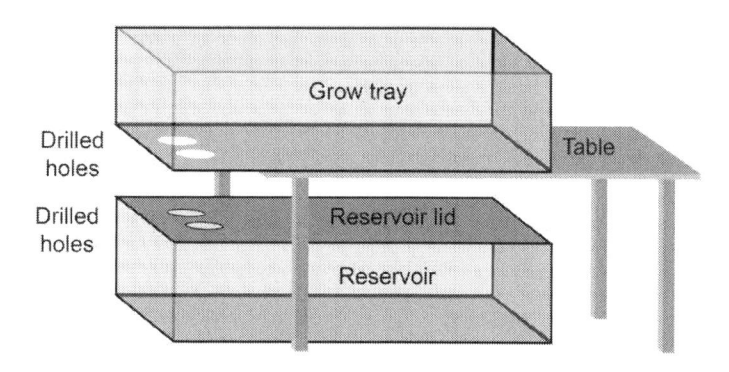

**Grow tray**

**Drilled holes**

**Table**

**Drilled holes**

**Reservoir lid**

**Reservoir**

7. Attach the fill fitting set to your inlet hole.
8. Cut a piece of hose to connect the inlet fitting and pump outlet, so they are bound together. The length of tubing needs to be long enough for the pump to sit at the bottom of the reservoir comfortably while the grow tray is on top. This will take some testing and you will need to adjust it to get it right. Cut off small pieces until it fits nicely. You may have to secure the tubing on both sides further with a zip tie. It should be tight.

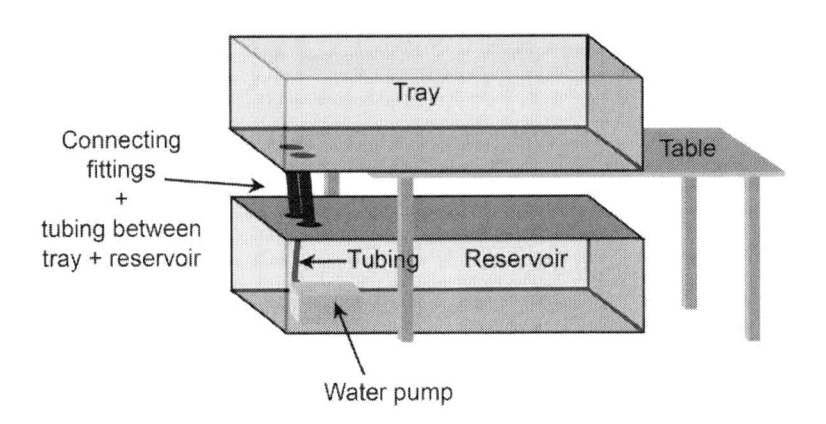

9. Arrange pump at the bottom of your reservoir.
10. Cut a piece of hose for your overflow. It needs to be long enough to be above your anticipated water flood height in the grow tray and long enough to reach into the reservoir but not touch the water. Fit the tubing into the overflow hole. Attach the overflow fitting to the top of the tubing so it is in the grow tray.
11. Run the cord from your pump through the notch in the reservoir lid so the plug is on the outside of your system.

12. Add 15 gallons of water to the reservoir or as much as you need for the number of plants you are growing. Mark on your reservoir the fill line so you can easily see how you are using and if/when you need to fill it again.
13. Add the necessary nutrients for the number of plants you are growing.
14. Rinse the clay pebbles until the water runs clean.
15. Fill the plant containers with the growing medium.
16. Put the containers in the grow tray.
17. Set up your timer and pump.
18. Put each seed in its' own germination starter cube, about 1/2" deep.
19. Put each germination starter cube with seed in a growing container, snuggling it down a little bit into the grow medium.
20. Pour water very carefully over the germination cubes so they are wet without being drenched.
21. Turn on your pumps. Set them up to run as often as needed for your growing medium and climate conditions.
22. Make sure everything is set up as it should be. The lights should be attached to your timer – make sure it is working right. The system timer should be set up to control the flood and drain.
23. DO NOT turn on the lights. For the first few days they seeds need to be in the dark to germinate.

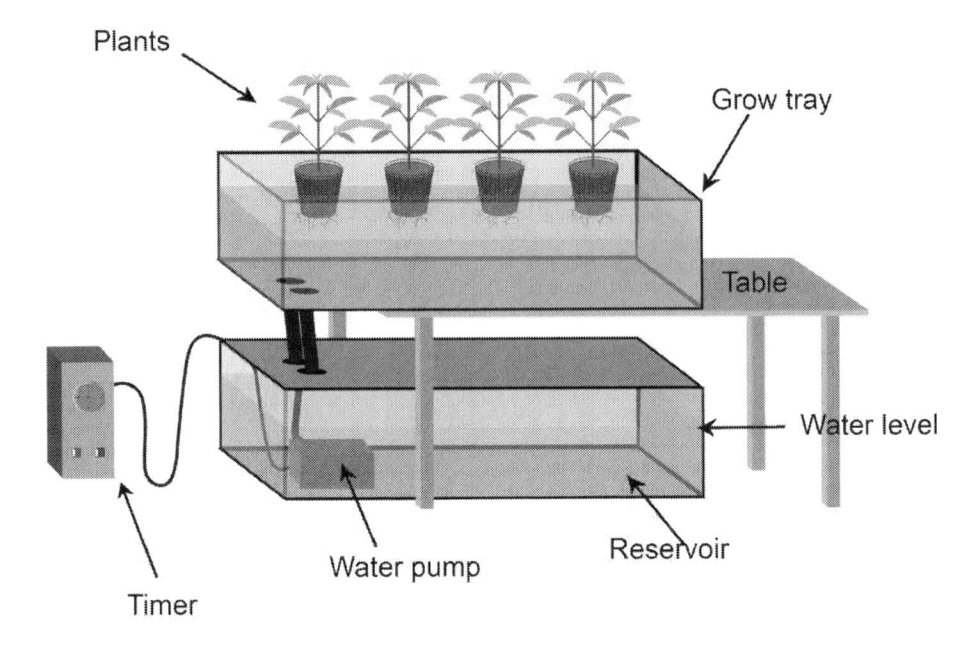

*Diagram: Hydroponic flood and drain system showing Plants, Grow tray, Table, Water level, Reservoir, Water pump, and Timer.*

### How Often to Run Pumps

I wish I could tell you an exact schedule, however, there are too many variables involved, including the climate you live in and which stage the plants are in. This is a basic guide and you will need to adapt it based your own circumstances. It will likely take some constant, frequent monitoring and testing the first time you do this system to ensure all is going well. In general, the amount of floodings ranges from 1-6 times per day.

- Slow draining mediums (rockwool) – 2x/day
- Fast draining mediums (clay pellets) – 3x/day
- Cool or humid environments – 2x/day
- Warm environments – 3x/day
- Hot/Dry environments – 4x/day

During the vegetative stage, the plants will need to be flooded 1x more than usual. In the flowering stage, they will remain at the normal number of floodings.

Very Important ---> Do not do the floodings while the plants are sleeping during the dark hours. Any floodings need to be done while the lights are on. This is to keep the regular day/night schedule as perfect as possible. For example, if your plants are in the flowering stage and getting flooded 3x/day, those 3 times will need to be spread out during the 12 hours of light.

Other things that can affect the amount of floodings you need to do per day include a large grow tray that takes longer to fill and/or a slow pump.

Each flooding should last 15 minutes and then the draining another 15 minutes.

## *Step #2 – Germination*

1. Check the plants daily! Check the set-up. Make sure the germination cubes are staying wet and that the pump timings are working correctly.
2. While your plants are getting used to their new system, it is recommended that you water them from the top for a few days so the roots don't dry out.
3. Maintain a pH between 5.5 and 6.3.
4. Do not turn on the lights until the seedlings burst from the surface of the germination cube.
5. Check the water level in your reservoir. The plants won't be using a whole lot just yet but it is good to get into the habit of constantly monitoring to make sure there is enough.
6. Make sure water is draining well and not pooling in the tray.
7. Check for blockages in the overflow tube.

## Step #3 – Seedling

1. Set light timer for an 18/24 light schedule.
2. Use blue-wavelength lights during this stage. [see lighting information]
3. Continue to check connections, pH levels, light, humidity, and equipment.
4. If the seedling leaves start to yellow or turn brown, cut back the amount of nutrients you are giving them. Drain and replace the water if this is an issue. Alternately, if the leaves are pale but the pH is correct, increase the amount of nutrients.
5. The plants will be in this stage for 2-3 weeks until they start growing bigger leaves. [see cannabis plant growing stages for more details]
6. Change the nutrient-enriched water every 7 days.
7. Keep the temperature around 75 degrees for the rest of the growing time. Bacteria can flourish in water reservoirs and high temperatures will encourage the bacteria to grow. There are beneficial bacteria products on the market that can be used to get rid of the bad stuff and introduce good ones.
8. Make sure water is draining well and not pooling in the tray.
9. Check for blockages in the overflow tube.

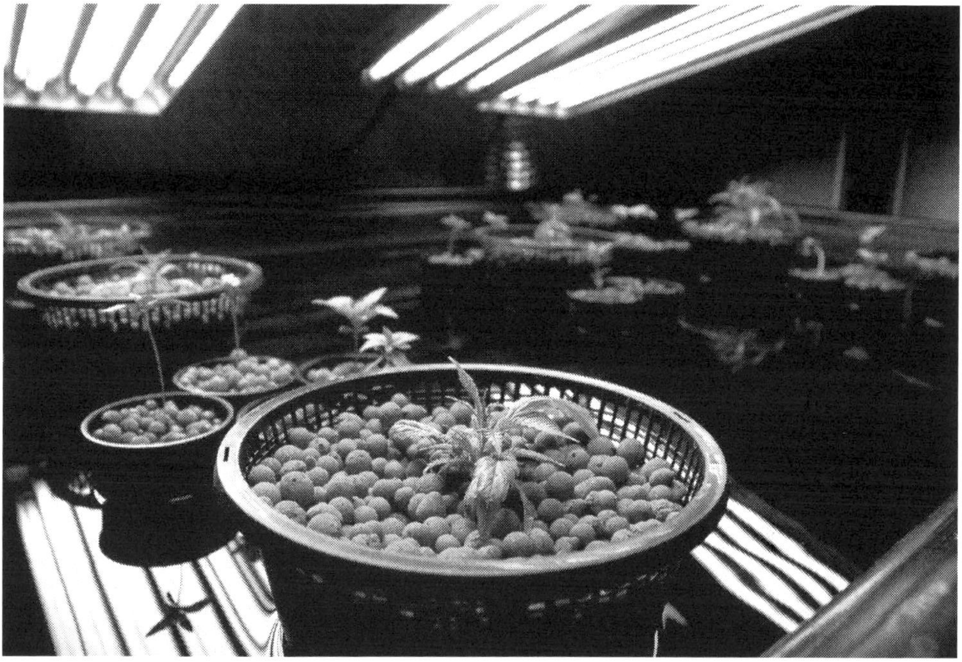

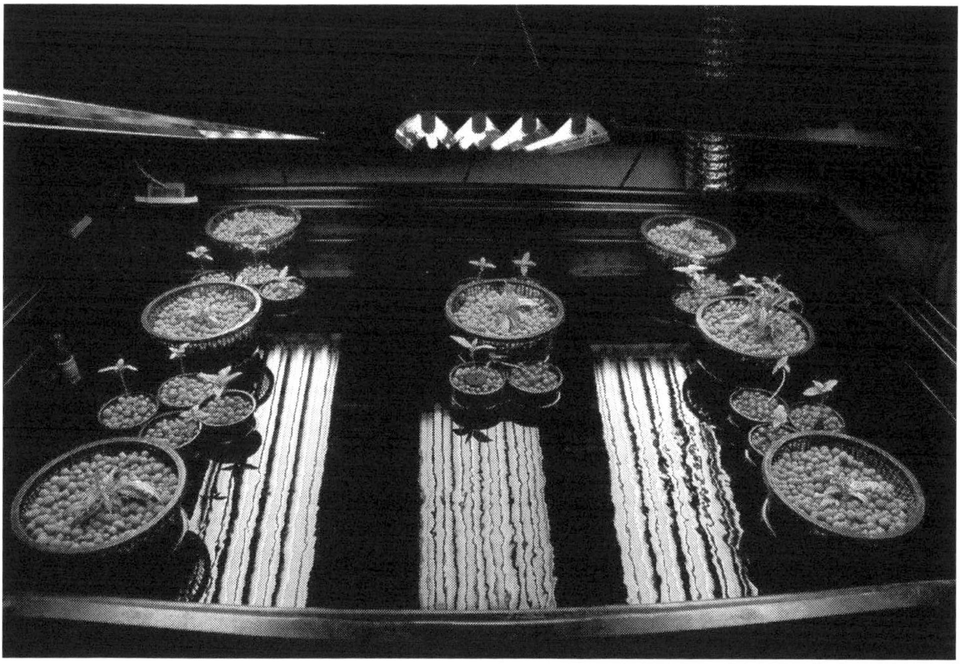

## *Step #4 – Vegetative Stage*

The amount of time the plants need in this stage will depend on the type and strain of the plants. There is no clear-cut time-period. In general, it is around 2-3 weeks.

1. Keep the light schedule at 18/24.
2. Increase the number of floodings by one.
3. Keep the blue-wavelength lights.
4. As the plants grow, you may need to adjust your lights and move them higher up so they aren't too close to the leaves and burning them.
5. Change the nutrient-enriched water every 7 days being mindful of any changes in leaf color and reducing/increasing nutrient levels as needed.
6. The plants are growing rapidly at this point and therefore using more water. Check water levels more frequently to make sure they have enough. Refill as needed.
7. Check the pH regularly.
8. Check the water for bacteria growth, cloudiness, and smells. Check the roots for root rot.
9. Monitor equipment.
10. Make sure water is draining well and not pooling in the tray.
11. Check for blockages in the overflow tube.

## *Step #5 – Flowering Stage*

As with the vegetative stage, the amount of time a plant will flower before being ready to harvest is dependent on variety and strain. This stage is the longest and will last from 4-12 weeks.

1. Change the light schedule to 12/12.
2. Decrease the number of floodings by one.

3. Switch to an orange-red wavelength lighting system.
4. Change the nutrient-enriched water every 7 days or as needed. Switch to a flowering nutrient formula for this stage.
5. Check the pH regularly.
6. Check the roots of your plants for any color changes – white is great, brown or slimy is bad.
7. Investigate for male/female/hermaphrodite plants! Remove any that aren't female.
8. Make sure water is draining well and not pooling in the tray.
9. Check for blockages in the overflow tube.

## *Step #6 – Harvest*

1. Refer to the harvesting section to know the appropriate time to harvest.

**TIP**

Have an extra batch of nutrient-enriched water on hand. Use it to top off your reservoir.

Change entire reservoir every 7 days (do not let roots dry out!)

## Growing Medium

The grow tray, or grow containers, need to be filled with a medium to support the plants. Everyone has their own preference for growing mediums. Medium options include expanded clay pebbles (hydroton) granulated rockwool, vermiculite, perlite, coconut fiber, and gravel. Each medium has different absorbent capabilities and so the time between floodings will need to be adjusted depending on which one you use.

A common choice is expanded clay pebbles. Clay pebbles provide great support and plant roots can go easily through them. If you are setting the plants directly in the grow tray instead of in individual containers, you will want to use this medium. On their own, clay pebbles don't hold much water, so you'll need to flood your tray approximately every 2 hours.

Clay pebbles can be mixed 50/50 with diatomite which gives the plants more nutrition. If diatomite is used, you'll need to reduce the irrigation frequency because it is more absorbent than clay pebbles.

Another suggestion is a 50/50 mix of coconut fiber and perlite, with two inches of clay pebbles on the bottom. This combination provides secure holding for the seedlings, moisture retention, and aeration. Putting the clay pebbles at the bottom prevents the other medium from getting washed away when the grow tray is flooded.

Your growing medium should be allowed to dry out well in-between flooding. This encourages your plants to flower. A constantly over-wet medium will produce lots of green foliage instead of producing large buds and flower.

## Fill/Drain Overflow Fitting Kit

These are readily available online or at your local home and garden store. They are inexpensive and consist of two hard plastic threaded pieces that will be attached to your grow tray.

They come in several sizes and the size of your tubing will need to match your fittings. Many companies sell inexpensive Ebb and Flow fittings sets.

The smaller piece of the kit is the for the inlet. It allows water to be pumped up into the grow tray. The longer piece is for the overflow tube. It has slits around the threaded top that allow the water to flow back into the reservoir. The overflow drain is extremely important because without it, if your pump malfunctions, water could overflow out of your grow table.

## Pump

The pump needs to be strong enough to take the water from the reservoir to the grow tray without being so strong that it turns your water into a fountain. Pumps usually have listed on them how high they will pump. This is measured in HEAD, so if a pump is rated at 3 feet of HEAD, then it will pump 3 feet. If the pump only has a PSI (pounds per square inch) rating, you'll need to multiply that number by 2.31 to get the HEAD. A good rule of thumb is to get a pump with a HEAD rating at least double of what you need.

## Tubing

The size of your tubing should match the size of your Fill/Drain fittings and your pump fitting. How much you need will depend on the set-up of your system and how far away the reservoir is from your grow tray. Clear irrigation tubing is recommended.

## Timer

There are two timer options: segmental (or mechanical) and digital.

A segmental timer is set to go off at specific time segments. For example, it can be set for every 20 minutes, or every 6 hours, or whatever space of time you want in-between your flooding. The benefits of this type of timer are that it's less expensive than a digital one and it's much easier to set up. The downsides are that it is less accurate than a digital timer, some of them have a loud ticking noise that people find irritating, and if they get accidentally bumped into, their settings can get thrown off. In addition, if the power goes off, the programming gets upset. The timer shuts off when the power goes off and turns back on when the power returns without accounting for the time it wasn't working. This can severely mess up your cycles.

With a digital timer, you can set the specific time each day that the timer goes off. For example, every morning at 8 a.m. and every evening at 10 p.m. Digital timers are more precise than segmental ones, however, there are some downsides. They are much more expensive and can be a terrible pain to set up. The upsides of a digital timer are numerous. They usually have a backup battery, so if the power goes out, it won't mess up your cycles. You can set them in many different ways that aren't possible with a segmental timer. They can be set to do things on specific days of the week, or combination of days, at specific times, and for very precise amounts of time. With a digital timer, you can set your flood times to smaller increments than with a segmental timer.

A digital timer is preferred over a segmental one. With a digital timer, you will have more control over your irrigation times.

A general purpose 15-amp timer is adequate for this use. 10-amp timers often burn out so it is recommended that you spend a little extra money on the 15-amp. An indoor/outdoor timer is also recommended because they are grounded and safer to use around water.

As with anything dealing with electricity, please exercise caution when setting up your timers. It is important not to overload your sockets or power outputs; doing so can have very bad consequences. Please pay very close attention to the amps!

# Caring for Hydroponic Marijuana

As with any garden venture, your hydroponic system will require maintenance to keep your plants healthy and your system operating well. You won't have to weed plants beds or mess with soil. Instead, you'll have to keep a close eye on a number of factors: temperature, water level, nutrient level, and cleanliness. Maintaining each of these factors is vital to the healthy growth of your crop. Monitor your system on a regular basis to make sure everything is working properly.

## Cleanliness

- Clean the grow space before you set up your system. Clean your grow boxes, reservoirs, grow pots and any other equipment you are using. This is best done with a 10% bleach solution.
- Any leaves, flowers, or organic matter that comes off your plants should be removed immediately. Don't leave it lying around. This will encourage pests and diseases to take hold, as they thrive on dead plant matter.

## Nutrient Solution

- It is recommended that you completely change out the nutrient water solution in your reservoir weekly. In some cases, it's ok to just top off the water. However, if you have an imbalance of micronutrients or a disease is trying to take hold, a top-off won't prevent it.

## Watering

- This is the most common question asked by new hydroponic growers and the most difficult to answer. The answer is completely dependent on what kind of system you have, what plants you are growing, the growing medium, surrounding temperature, etc. Here's the rule of thumb: Water enough to keep the roots wet, but not so much that they remain saturated.

- If you notice the growing medium and roots getting dry between watering cycles, increase the irrigation frequency. If they seem to be wet all the time, decrease the frequency. The frequency can be adjusted as many times as you need until you have it correct for your system. Remember that as your plants grow, their water needs will change.

- In general, there is no need to water at night. Plants absorb the most water when it is light out. They don't use much during the dark hours. When you set up your timer, plan the irrigation cycles for the daylight hours. If you notice that your plants are getting dry at night, add a nighttime watering cycle as well.

## Reservoir Temperature

- The temperature of the water in your reservoir should be around 70F. If you struggle to maintain this temperature, consider getting a heating mat and placing it below the reservoir. Alternately, you can put a heating element inside the reservoir. If you have a small reservoir, an aquarium heater will work well.

- If the temperature is too hot, try adding clean ice packs to the reservoir. Wrapping the reservoir in foil to deflect heat is another option, and it is both easy and inexpensive. If these methods don't work, you can purchase a water chiller. This is a coiled element that cools water. It can be installed in the reservoir to keep the temperature down.

## Humidity

- Humidity and temperature are not the same thing. They serve separate purposes and both need to be monitored closely. Your plant's needs will change over time. Keep this in mind when checking temperature and humidity levels. Different types of plants also have different needs.

- During the initial growth stage of a seedling, the humidity needs to be above 80%. This is only for when the seeds are germinating. After this, the humidity should be lowered to promote plant growth.

- Humidity can be hard to control. However, as you read in the pests and diseases section, it is extremely important. Too much humidity can be devastating for your plants. Too little can cause your plant to dry out. One of the best pieces of advice regarding humidity is to get a hygrometer for your grow space!

- Seasonal temperatures where you live can affect the humidity of your grow space, even if it is indoors. The ventilation in your space will also have a huge impact on the humidity. Check humidity on a regular basis to account for natural fluctuations.

- If you need to add humidity, get a vaporizer or humidifier. Another option, although not a great one, is to use a spray bottle and spray water around the room. It isn't a great option because it will get all your equipment wet as well. If you need to decrease the humidity, the best option is to increase ventilation. Increased air flow will sweep away excess moisture in the air. A simple fan (or two or three) will work wonders. Dehumidifiers or air conditioners also do an excellent job of reducing humidity.

- Humidity is also affected by the number of plants being grown and how densely they are arranged. Many plants close to one another will create a windbreak that doesn't allow fresh air to flow through. If the plants are spaced too closely together, the water vapor they exude will have nowhere to go.
- If you'd like to get a little fancier, you can hook up a hygrometer to a fan and have it run automatically when it senses increased humidity.

## Inspect the Equipment

- Pumps, timers, aerators, tubing, and connectors can all fail. Plus, it can take hours or days before your plants show signs of malfunctioning equipment. Checking your equipment regularly will prevent situations before they reach challenging proportions.

## Look at your Plants!

- Really look at them. Look under the leaves, examine the roots, and take notice of any abnormalities on a day-to-day basis. Monitor growth patterns. If you are keeping a close eye on them, you will notice when things look off or when something goes wrong.
- Check the Water Levels Regularly Test the Nutrient Levels and pH regularly. Every 3-4 days at a minimum. Every day is better.

## Take Notes!

Check on your plants. Take note of how much nutrient solution they are using, how big they are growing, which nutrients you are using, and how much water they are getting if they're on a timer. You won't regret this, I promise. After you have completed one grow cycle, it helps 100-fold with your next cycle to have detailed notes of what worked and what didn't, as well as any problems that were encountered and how they were overcome.

## Change One Thing at a Time!

When you are making adjustments to your system, do only one thing at a time. If you change multiple things, it becomes hard to know exactly what fixed the problem. And, if your changes cause another problem, it will be difficult to ascertain exactly why. Make changes in increments. Record the results each time.

# Harvesting, Drying, and Curing of your Hydroponic Marijuana Plant

Knowing when to harvest is just as important as knowing how to grow the plants. If you harvest too soon, the potency of the marijuana will not be at its peak and yields will be smaller. That is no good! If you harvest too late, THC amounts decrease while CBD amounts increase. This may be what you want, but if it isn't, then it will be a possibly unwelcome occurrence.

There are two methods to identifying the correct harvest time, the Pistil Method and the Trichome Method. They each have their benefits and downsides. Both are easy and are best used in conjunction with each other to determine if your plants are ready.

There is another step that should be done before the harvest, flushing. This step is optional, yet highly recommended to get the best quality cannabis.

## Flushing

This technique is simple and easy to do. It doesn't require any special tools, just some understanding of the growing process so you can determine the appropriate time. Flushing removes any extra nutrients from out of the buds. If it is done too soon, however, it can negatively affect the quality and yield of your plants.

Flushing is the process of providing your plants with plain water without nutrients for a period of time before the harvest. The time can range from a few days up to 2 weeks, depending on the plants, the system being used, and on the grower. Water is provided in the same way that is normally done with your system, the nutrients are simply omitted.

The plants still need to have the appropriate pH, however, which may mean adding a pH Up or Down formula. The pH Up/Down products don't have nutrients so they are ok. Plus, a pH that is too high or too low will make salts and aluminum more available to your plant and you don't want that. Do not neglect to maintain the pH levels even during flushing.

## *Flushing Steps*

1. Figure out the expected harvest window. [see methods listed below to determine when the plants will be ready to harvest]
2. Plan to flush out the system for 2-3 days before the harvest.
3. Change out all the system in the reservoir with plain water. Do not add the nutrients or any other supplements except pH Up/Down products if needed. Do not add any more water than you normally would – the plants can get "overwatered".
4. Check for too much yellowing of plants. They will lose some green color during the flush. The plants should be harvested before the leaves on the buds turn yellow.
5. Harvest!

## *Clearing/Leaching Products for Flushing*

There are some products on the market that assist in removing excess salts and minerals. These can be added to the water during flushing if desired. These products are designed to help flush the system although they usually are not necessary. If you have been feeding your plants the recommended amount of nutrients, they won't need this. If you've been feeding them extra nutrients, they could benefit from the addition of a clearing solution.

### *Flushing Too Early*

The growth of your plant will be stunted if you flush too early. Make sure you have used the harvesting methods below to determine you are doing it at the right time. Since the flush happens just a few days before you harvest this shouldn't be an issue. The best thing to do is wait until are actually ready to be harvested and then flush them. This way you aren't interrupting the grow process and it only adds a few more days on.

**Effects of Flushing Too Early**

1. Stunted bud growth.
2. Reduced yields.
3. Lower potency of buds.
4. Unsightly appearance due to yellowing which can lead others to think it is poor quality even if it isn't.

## Harvesting – Are My Plants Ready?

### *Pistil Method*

The pistils on a cannabis plant are the hairs that stick up out of the bud. The hairs start out white and darken as they grow. Wait until at least half the white hairs have darkened and curled before harvesting. It can take weeks of watching before you see this occur. Be patient!

If you harvest when 60-70% of the pistils have darkened, you will get the highest level of THC. If you harvest when 70-80% of the hairs have darkened, some of the THC will have turned into CBN (cannabinol, which has sedative properties).

This method isn't exact since strains can look quite different and be hard to decipher. There are some strains in which the pistils stay mostly white even when they are ready to harvest. The only way to know is to talk to someone who has grown the same strain. An online search may be helpful too since growers like to post pictures of their harvests. You can find out what their plants looked like at harvest time.

### *Trichome Method*

This method is much more accurate than the Pistil Method. It doesn't require any super special equipment, just a magnifying glass or microscope. In this method, you will look closely at the trichomes on the buds. Trichomes are mushroom-like looking growths and are also called resin glands. They are the crystal-like substance that accumulates on the bud and leaves and makes it sticky.

Look for the trichomes with a little ball on top that look like a mushroom head. THC gathers in these little balls and is what makes it potent. There will be some trichomes without the little ball on top and those can be ignored as they don't affect potency.

A magnifying glass or microscope is needed to see the trichomes as they are very difficult to see with the naked eye.

The trichomes will change from clear to cloudy as they develop. When the trichomes are half clear and half cloudy, they are still growing and not quite fully developed. A harvest done at this time will produce cannabis that gives a more energetic high. The ideal time to harvest is when all the trichomes are cloudy (or milky). This is when the highest levels of THC are present. Cannabis harvested at this time will give the most potent high and have the deepest pain-relieving effects. If allowed to continue growing, the trichomes will turn an amber yellow color. At this stage, the THC will be less and the CBN will be higher which gives a more relaxing and narcotic-like high.

# Why Are My Plants Taking So Long To Mature?

So, you've had your plants in the flowering stage and it seems to be taking much longer than estimated for them to be ready to harvest. There are a number of reasons this can happen. And, there are some ways you can speed up the harvest.

### *Strain/Type*

As with all plants, not all strains perform the same. There are just some that take a lot longer than others. Some strains are labeled "lazy" because for a long time the buds won't look ready and then all of a sudden they will. It can feel like it happened overnight. Check your plants regularly and you may be pleasantly surprised to see them ready to go one day. These lazy plants are one of the main reasons you don't ever want to harvest too early. You may think they've grown all they are going to and then, boom, they grow wildly in a few days.

## Expectations

A seed source or breeder of the strain you are growing can give you the estimated flowering time. The time they give you, however, will be based on the time the flowers first start appearing. It's not the time from when you first switched to a 12-12 light schedule. That can make a huge difference! A general rule of thumb is to add 2 weeks on to the estimated time from the breeder.

Even with that adjustment, marijuana plants generally take longer to mature than the breeder indicates. This is due to several circumstances, mostly that the plants are technically ready for harvest at that earlier date even if they are not at the peak of their maturity.

## Heat & Light Stress

Too much heat and lights that are too bright can stress out your marijuana plants. When they are stressed out, they will keep producing new growth which takes away from developing already grown buds.

A sure sign of heat or light stress is yellow or burned leaves on the top of your plants. Additionally, you will likely see more white pistils growing out of the buds nearest your lights. The plant is trying to produce more buds that aren't stressed out. When it comes time to harvest, don't take into account the trichomes of any of these new buds as they will not be good indicators. Only use the older buds to determine if the plant is ready to harvest.

If you see this happening, make sure to fix and/or adjust the light and heat in your grow room.

### *Regression*

If your plants are getting light during the 12-hour time-period they are meant to be in the dark, they can revert back to the vegetative state. Even just a small amount of light can be enough to trigger the plants – a light leak or even small indicator light can be enough to cause this.

When this happens, the buds stop maturing and if they aren't forced back into flowering mode as soon as possible, the buds will turn brown and die. The appearance of new round or smooth leaves on the buds is a sign the plant is regressing to the vegetative state.

## Tips to Get Buds to Mature Faster

1. Reduce the light schedule. Giving the plants more hours of darkness will make them think it's winter which translates to 'time to mature'. Try a 10-14 light schedule or an 8-16 schedule.

    - You will get fewer buds if you reduce the hours of light. A small change, like 14-10, shouldn't make a huge difference but any more than that definitely can.

2. Make sure the darkness is completely dark. Check the entirety of your grow room to make sure no light is sneaking in.
3. Lower the temperature, light, and humidity. This is a method that many growers use to simulate the natural environment. Imitating the cold, dry weather of fall and winter can trigger the plants into maturing faster.
4. Supplements. There are special supplements you can give your plants to bring them to maturity quicker.
5. Be patient! Sometimes, all it comes down to is exercising a little patience and waiting for the plants to mature in their own time.

## Signs to Harvest Immediately

There are times when the trichomes and pistils don't seem to be how you want them but you should still harvest the plants anyways. These cases usually involve a sick or struggling plant and chances are they are not going to meet all the ready signs even if you wait.

1. Brown or burnt buds. If the buds look toasted or are developing brown spots, harvest them right away. Waiting will likely mean they will denigrate in potency.
2. Plant is dead. If the plant has lost all its leaves, it isn't going to grow or mature anymore and should be harvested straight away. In fact, if you wait too long the leaves can turn yellow and then the buds can turn yellow.
3. It's a hermie. Hermaphrodite plants are a problem because they can self-pollinate and pollinate your other plants. Pollination brings seeds which are not good for the quality of your harvest. Remove these plants from your room and harvest right away. Be super super careful moving a hermaphrodite plant. Cover it with a plastic bag first. Even if you can't see any pollen, it can be there and if you aren't careful you can contaminate the entire room.
4. Bud rot. If you see the symptoms of this disease, remove the plant immediately as it can infect the others. It can infect the others very quickly too, often overnight, so you might want to consider harvesting your entire crop so you don't lose it all.

## Harvesting Cannabis, Step By Step

1. Cut down the plant
2. Trim away the extra leaves
3. Start drying the buds

4. Let the buds dry until they feel dry to the touch (3-10 days)
5. Put the buds in glass jars
6. Let buds cure in glass jars (1-3 weeks)

**Equipment Needed For Harvesting, Drying, and Curing**

- Pruning scissors or other implement to cut down plants.
- Disposable gloves. Otherwise, your hands will get covered with sticky resin.
- Drying rack or other set-up to dry the buds. A clothes hanger can work well. A string strung across an open space. Get as creative as you like.
- Wide mouth glass jars, 1-quart size (32oz)
- Hygrometer. This isn't absolutely necessary but it's nice to have on hand to check the humidity inside the glass jars.
- Humidpaks. Another optional item. There are ones designed specifically for storing cannabis so it doesn't dry out.
- Equipment to keep desired temperature and humidity (fan, air conditioner, dehumidifier, humidifier, heater)

**1. Cut down the Plant**

The plants can be cut down at the base and then hung upside-down as whole plants. Alternately, the branches can be cut off and hung individually. Or, the individual buds can be cut off and laid out to dry. There is no best choice here; all these options will work well, it is entirely up to your personal preference.

**2. Trim Away the Extra Leaves**

All the big fan leaves should be trimmed away. The extra leafy material can make the buds harsher to smoke. Trimming the leaves also makes for a prettier bud. Aesthetics can mean a lot!

If you live in a humid area, cutting off as many of the fan leaves as possible will speed up the drying process. If you live in a drier area, leaving some fan leaves is recommended to slow down the drying process. Drying too quickly is also an issue since it doesn't give the buds time to develop their full flavor and potency.

## 3. Start Drying the Buds

It would be great if the harvest was the last step in growing cannabis; however, there is still one more step. And, while it is one you don't have to do, it is one that you really shouldn't skip. The curing process is a way of drying the buds so they keep better as well as reducing the harshness of the flavor and increasing potency. Uncured buds are weaker and less flavorful. Basically, if you have taken all the effort to grow good cannabis, it would be a shame to not let it achieve its full potential.

Ideal Drying Room Temperature – 70F with 50% humidity.

Ideal Curing Room Temperature – 70F with 58-56% humidity.

**Why Dry & Cure Cannabis?**
- Subtle flavors are brought out
- Harshness is reduced (less coughing and headaches when smoking)
- Removes the "fresh cut grass" smell of newly harvested marijuana
- Dramatically improves the taste through the breakdown of chlorophyll

## How to Dry Cannabis

The curing process begins the moment you cut down your plant. Do not wait to take care of your plants. Be ready to start the drying process as soon as they are harvested.

A slow drying process is best. Any time you speed it up, you are lessening the original benefits of drying. Do not use an oven or microwave to speed up the drying process! The end result will taste very bad.

Set up your drying buds in a location where you can check on them easily. They should be inspected every day to make sure they are drying, no mold is growing, and to check their progress.

## Ways to Dry the Harvest

**Hang them upside down.**

The easiest way to dry your plants is to hang them upside-down until the small stems snap when you bend them. At this point, the buds should just pop off the plant.

**Use a drying rack.**

A drying rack is another great option and quickens the drying process, though not so fast as to be detrimental. A rack only holds the buds and is the best option for humid locations. They are also great if you are drying in a small space.

**Lay out on cardboard.**

Laying out the buds on cardboard or another flat material is an easy method but not recommended. Although in a humid location, it can be a good option. The buds will leave wet spots on the cardboard and the buds themselves will be flattened by lying on a flat space. In a humid environment, the cardboard can be a great way to pull water quickly out of the buds. With this method, the buds will need to be rotated every few hours so they dry evenly.

**Drying in Humid Locations**

If you live in a humid location (over 60% humidity), then you may encounter problems with mold as you are drying your cannabis harvest. Many growers in humid environments separate the buds from the branches after harvesting to reduce the chances of mold. Mold grows when moisture has a chance to build up and sit for a period of time. An entire plant hanging upside-down will be moist for a long time since its surface area is so tight. All parts of the buds are not exposed to the air, branches and leaves block it. You want your buds to have their whole surface exposed to the air so they can dry.

## *4. Let Buds Dry Until They Feel Dry to the Touch*

The drying period should take between 3-10 days. If they dry faster than this, they have dried too fast. It's ok if that's the case – we all learn from experience and no environment is the same. Next time you can amend the method. The way to know the buds are dry is that you will be able to snap off the smallest ones with your fingers. Also, the smaller stems will easily break in half. The larger stems will still bend. It is important that the larger stems still be bendy since this means there is still some moisture left which is needed for the curing process. If the larger stems snap in half, the buds are over-dried. It's not terrible if this happens, however, it means the curing process will take longer and your buds will not be at the peak of their quality.

If you removed the buds from the stems during the trimming process, check the outside of the buds for dryness. As soon as they feel dry, start jarring them.

Stopping the drying process at the correct time is very important. The buds need some moisture to assist in the curing process, however, too wet or too dry will cause problems during the curing. Buds that are too dry without any bendy stems or moisture at all will take forever to cure. Buds that are too moist and still damp or moist to the touch will grow mold.

## *5. Put the Buds in Glass Jars*

Jars are used to store the buds because they create a controlled environment. Curing demands a specific temperature and humidity. The room temperature should be around 70F and the humidity between 60-65%. Buds that have been moved from drying to curing while the small stems snap and the big stems still bend will create their own ideal humidity within the jar.

If the humidity is too low, the buds will start to disintegrate into crumbly bits in your hands. If the humidity is too high, mold and bacteria can develop. The environment where you live will have a lot of power in how well the drying and curing process goes. Be sure to check local temperatures, humidity levels, and such before you begin the process.

For the best results, use wide-mouth quart glass jars with a good seal. This is specifically because the size and shape do matter for proper curing to happen. A larger jar can develop mold easier. Do not use jars that have rubber seals. A jar without good sealing won't cure the buds as desired. One jar will hold approximately one ounce of dried buds. These jars are relatively easy to find online or in garden and home supply stores. It may seem odd to be so specific about what type of jar to use but I don't want you to have any problems with your crop now that you've gotten this far!

*Jarring and Curing Steps*

1. Fill each jar 75% full

    - There needs to be air still in the jar. Do not stuff the jars all the way full. They need room to move around and air needs to be able to circulate.

    - If the buds stick together, they need more drying time as they are still too wet. Remove them from the jars and continue the drying process. Wet, sticky, buds encourage mold so be ultra careful about this. Mold and bacteria love wet conditions and can make your cannabis unsafe to use.

2. Check jars every 24 hours (minimally) for 1-2 weeks

    - For the first week, it's good to check the jars 2-3x/day but once a day will be good too. This is to make sure no mold is growing and to give the buds fresh air which they need for the curing process.

    - The buds need fresh air for about 1 minute each day. Opening and closing the jars once is enough for them to get the fresh air they need.

    - If an ammonia smell comes from your jar of buds, the buds are too wet and bad bacteria are starting to take hold. Leave the lid off the jar until the buds are drier, if this happens.

    - When the buds begin smelling like the regular cannabis smell, it means they are curing well.

    - Check the humidity levels with a hygrometer (recommended but not absolutely necessary)

    - Buds will sweat somewhat in the jars. The moisture that was in the middle of the bud is being drawn out and is now on the surface of the bud. This can make originally dry buds feel wet. If this happens, leave the lids off those jars until the buds are dry to the touch again.

- Shake the jar around to move the buds and make sure none are sticking in clumps.
3. After the first 2 weeks, open jars 1-2x/week only.
4. After 4 weeks, open the jars 1x/month for 5 months [total curing time – 6 months].

## Bud Curing Quick Reference

→ If the buds feel wet, remove the buds from the jar and let them sit for 12-24 hours until they feel dry again.

→ If the buds feel damp, leave them in the jar with the lid off for 2-4 hours until they feel dry again.

→ If the buds feel dry, they are doing great! Keep up the good work.

→ If the buds feel brittle or crumbly, they are too dry and should be left alone or have a humidifier pak added.

The reason for checking frequently, especially during the first week, is because mold and bacteria can take hold quite fast. The ideal bud texture is slightly sticky on the fingers. They should not form big clumps when you shake the jars and should move individually.

No wet buds should touch each other and if they feel damp to the touch at all, you need to remove them from the jars, separate them, and let them dry out again.

Moist (not wet) buds won't all stick together but some might clump a bit when you shake your jars. A few hours with the lid off the jar should solve this problem.

Crumbly, slightly disintegrating buds are too dry. This isn't as bad as too wet since no mold will grow. It will just take a lot longer for the buds to finish curing. Over-dried buds can be rehydrated, however, you need to be careful doing this and only use approved rehydrators. The risk of mold is increased during rehydration. Any type of organic addition, like an orange peel, can greatly increase the chances of mold growing. A humidpak can do this for you and there are options available online for them.

Humidpaks are added to jars of curing bud to maintain a humidity level. These are added to prevent the humidity from getting too low. Some humidpaks are made specifically for curing marijuana and are a great tool for having a successful curing process. They can be used as a tool to maintain a good humidity level even when there are no issues. They can also be added to the jars to rehydrate over-dried buds.

## *Storage*

After 6 months, the buds won't get much benefit from continued curing. At 3 months, they can be stored or they can be cured longer, it's up to you.

To store the buds for a few months, keep them in the glass jars in a dark, cool, environment.

To store the buds for more than 6 months, move the glass jars to your freezer. Or, vacuum seal them in plastic and put them in the freezer that way.

# Pests, Disease and Other Problems

## Pests

Pests can be a huge issue in an indoor grow situation. There aren't many pests that affect cannabis plants indoors, especially when compared to outdoor growing, but once they take hold it can be a lot harder to eradicate them. Cleaning an indoor grow space while the plants are still growing is time-consuming, problematic, and stressful for you and the plants. The best way to avoid this from happening is to take a few preventative measures.

### *Preventative Measures*

1. Seal off the room before starting growing
2. Ensure the room is easy to clean
3. Sanitize the space before use

### *Whiteflies*

These are small, white bugs that feed on the plants' juices. They excrete a fluid while they eat which turns into mold. It's likely you will see the mold before the flies. Sticky bug traps will capture the adults in the grow area while a spray of neem oil on the leaves of the plants will kill the eggs and nymphs.

## Spider Mites

These very tiny bugs look like spiders except super small. They can be a variety of colors: red, yellow, and light green. They feed on the plant stems, weakening the entire plant. If you see leaves with yellow speckles on top, it is likely it is spider mites. You will see the evidence of them before you see the mites themselves since they are so small.

Spider mites like dry places and the best way to keep them away is to keep the humidity level above 50% as much as possible. An organic substance spray, Pyrethrin, is also good for treating spider mite infestations. The mites will move from plant to plant, so if you see evidence of them, isolate the infected plant(s) and treat it.

## *Thrips*

Another tiny insect that likes to suck on the plants' juices, thrips invade in large numbers. They will also eat flower petals. Signs of a thrip invasion include dark, brittle, leaves and flowers. Thrips can be scraped carefully off leaves and crushed. Insecticidal soap will also work to remove them. These insects breed quickly and have short lives so it's a good idea to treat your plants for several weeks even if you don't see them anymore. This ensures you interrupt their next hatching cycle.

### *Aphids*

Aphids attack plants that are weak or stressed out. Plants that have been over-fed are also a big target. They suck the sap out of leaves, buds, stems, and flowers without discretion. They can spread viral diseases from one plant to another so it is very important that you deal with these infestations as soon as possible.

Washing the leaves with water removes many of the bugs. Insecticidal soap will also work. To avoid these bugs from getting into your grow space, do not bring in tools or anything from outside which the bugs can piggyback on.

## Diseases

### *Root Rot*

Root rot is a real issue and a common problem. Plants can look completely healthy up until they die with root rot. So, be sure to monitor and don't hesitate to take action if you see any signs of it. Root rot kills plants! And, it spreads from one to the other and can do so quite quickly.

If you see odd bits floating in the reservoir water, notice a bad smell, or see the plant roots are brown, then you have root rot. If caught soon enough, the bad parts of the roots can be trimmed off. If not caught in time, remove the affected plant immediately and keep a very close eye on the others. Always, replace the reservoir water and include an additive that fights bacteria.

To prevent root rot from wanting to invade your plants, keep the water temperature below 72F. High water temps provide an ideal grow space for root rot. Do not over-feed your plants. High levels of nutrients that aren't being absorbed are also welcomed by root rot bacteria. Additionally, do not let light infiltrate your reservoir.

## *Powdery Mold*

A white powder appearing on the leaves is white powdery mold. Increase circulation by adding more fans and watch the humidity and temperature to make sure they are ideal. Powdery mold can be treated with specially made mold treatments.

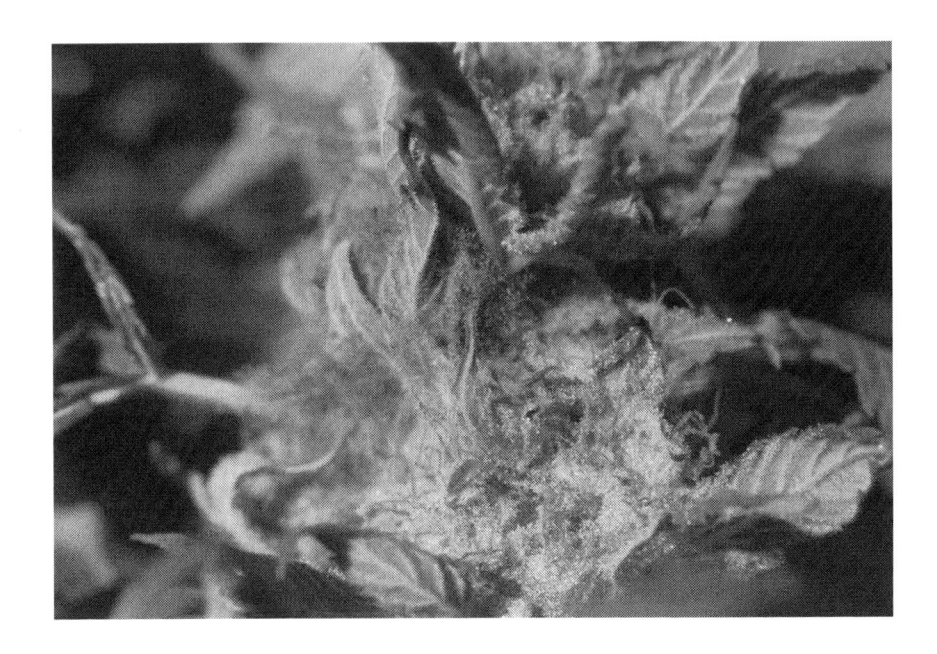

# Other Problems

### *Faded Leaf Color*

Check the pH in your reservoir; it is most likely off.

### *Yellow/Brown Leaves, Curled Tips (Nutrient Burn or Deficiency)*

This is the most common problem new growers encounter. It can be hard to determine exactly how much nutrients your plants need. Sure, the bottle or powder that you are using will tell you how much to add but it often isn't accurate. There are too many variables, like how many plants you are growing, the types of plants, the quality of your water, and the actual hydroponic set-up you are using. The amount of nutrients you add will need to be adjusted often during the first couple times you grow using hydroponics until you learn your system and plants better.

Nutrient burn happens when there are too many nutrients in the water. The cannabis plants are trying to take them all in and it's overwhelming them. Telltale signs of this are that the leaves will turn yellow or brown on the tips. If it isn't fixed, the leaves will continue to deteriorate and the entire leaf will become twisted and dry. Eventually, the growth of your plants will slow down significantly and this will negatively affect your end bud yields.

If this happens, drain the reservoir and add a new batch with fewer nutrients. The leaves that were affected initially won't go back to normal but the measures will prevent other leaves from turning brown.

On the side of the spectrum you can have nutrient deficiency causing problems with your plants Nutrient deficiencies will cause the leaves on your plant to change color, wilt away and eventually die. The plant typically appears pale or in different colored.

### *Less Water Absorption*

If you notice your plants aren't drinking as much water as they normally do, it is likely the pH is off. Check the pH and adjust it as necessary. If necessary, drain and replace the nutrient solution.

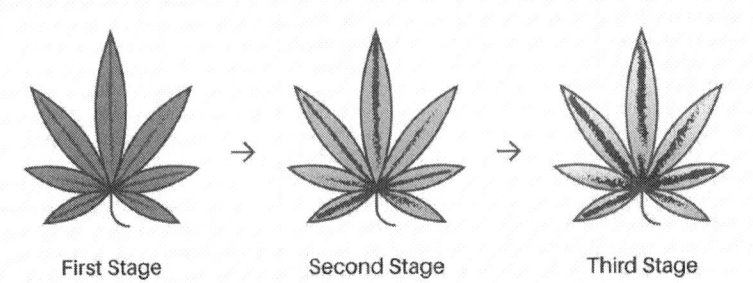

## Phosphorus Deficiency Symptoms

First Stage → Second Stage → Third Stage

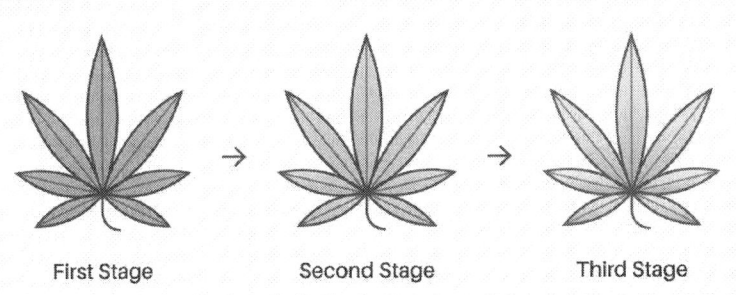

## Nitrogen Deficiency Symptoms

First Stage → Second Stage → Third Stage

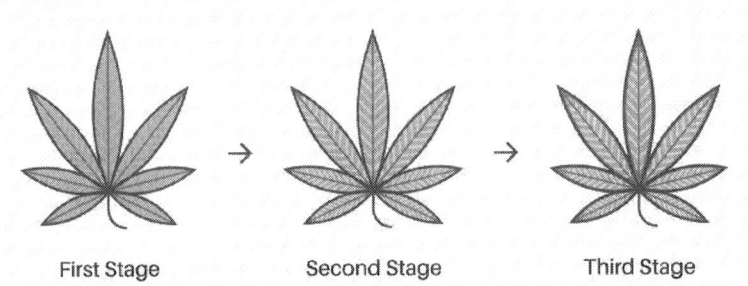

## Magnesium Deficiency Symptoms

First Stage → Second Stage → Third Stage

## Potassium Deficiency Symptoms

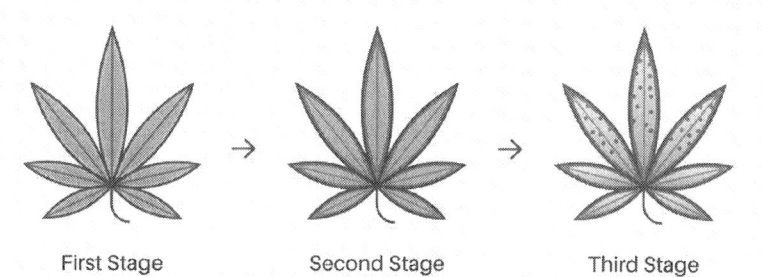

First Stage → Second Stage → Third Stage

## Sulfur Deficiency Symptoms

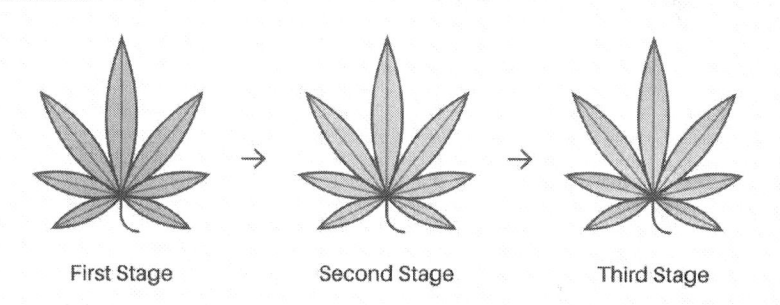

First Stage → Second Stage → Third Stage

## Zinc Deficiency Symptoms

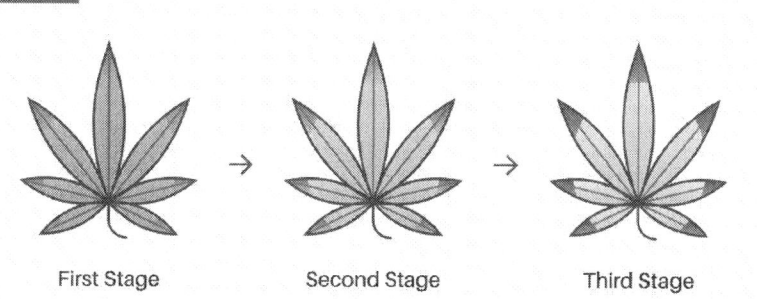

First Stage → Second Stage → Third Stage

# Conclusion

Whether you're new to hydroponics or an experienced hydroponic grower, using hydroponics to grow cannabis is a great choice. The systems are not too complicated to set up and the end yields are well worth the effort. For new growers, it will take some time to learn the intricacies specific to your growing situation but they aren't any more complicated than what you need to learn to grow with soil.

Hydroponics is especially great for growing cannabis because you get quicker harvest, can grow all year-round, and the yields are bigger. It is the best results for even the smallest amount of efforts and is making hydroponics the first choice for most cannabis growers.

# Review

If you enjoyed this book and found some benefit in reading this, I'd like to hear from you and hope that you could take one minute to post an honest review on Amazon. Your feedback really makes a difference.

I wish you all the best for your hydroponic project!

# About the Author

Richard's father was a keen gardener and that is where his interest in all natural things began. As a youngster, he enjoyed nothing better than helping his father in the garden.

Nowadays, he finds himself at the opposite end of life. Having had a satisfying career, he now has time to potter around in his garden and take care of his small homestead. Much of the food on his dinner table is homegrown. He likes to experiment with various gardening methods and find new ways to grow bountiful crops year-round.

He wants to share his knowledge and show how easy and rewarding it is to set up your own prosperous garden. In his opinion, you don't need a huge budget to get started. When you do get started, you will soon feel, and taste, the benefits of growing your own food.

Learn more about Richard Bray at

*amazon.com/author/richardbray*

Printed in Great Britain
by Amazon